GODS AND HEROES OF
THE GREEKS

By the same author

A HANDBOOK OF GREEK LITERATURE
A HANDBOOK OF GREEK MYTHOLOGY
A HANDBOOK OF LATIN LITERATURE

Gods and Heroes of the Greeks

H. J. ROSE, M.A., LL.D., F.B.A.

NEW ENGLISH LIBRARY
TIMES MIRROR

First published in Great Britain by Methuen & Co. Ltd. in 1957

*

FIRST NEL PAPERBACK EDITION SEPTEMBER 1974

NEL Books are published by The New English Library Limited from Barnard's Inn, Holborn, London E.C.1. Made and printed in Great Britain by C. Nicholls & Company Ltd

45002187 4

*To all the children
who like me to tell them stories*

CONTENTS

PREFACE

MY *Handbook of Greek Mythology* has met with a kind reception both in this country and abroad; but it has been suggested to me that it is rather too large, elaborate and expensive for those who want no more than an outline acquaintance with the subject, and perhaps especially for young students of language and literature in our schools and universities. The present work is an attempt to supply the needs of such readers. It is not a series of extracts from the larger book, but newly written, and while covering much the same ground as the *Handbook* it omits many of the less important stories and all the apparatus of reference to ancient authors and modern specialist treatises which that contains. I hope it will be found profitable and not uninteresting reading.

H. J. ROSE

I

INTRODUCTORY

Most peoples, though not all, have a store of traditional tales, which may remain oral till some anthropologist collects them and sets them down in print, or may be taken up into the native literature and provide material for poets and other imaginative writers, if the people in question progress so far as to express themselves in writing. Of all such inheritances of legend, that of Greece is the most famous, for it has been used not only by Greek writers but by those of ancient Rome and medieval and modern Europe. It is through the ancient authors, including several who wrote handbooks of the subject, that our information has been handed down. A modern, however, should not be content with repeating what those authors say, but should ask what manner of people they were who told the stories, how old they are, and what kind of stories they are.

The ancient Greeks, like all peoples who have made a great name for themselves, were a mixed people whose civilization was constructed from a wide variety of materials. From a very early date Greece proper was inhabited by folk of not very advanced culture, known to modern archaeologists who have studied their material remains as Thessalians and Helladics, because ruins of their settlements, tools and implements of their making, and so forth, have come to light partly in Thessaly, partly in the rest of Hellas, or Greece; the Thessalian culture being the earlier in date. Into their country came a people of unknown origin, whom it is convenient to call Achaians, that being one of Homer's names for them. These were in some ways more advanced, for they used horses, were tolerably well organized for war and peace, and had in them great possibilities of development. Their original home seems to have had a rather colder climate than the Mediterranean, which does not mean that they must have come, as once was hastily concluded, from central or northern Europe. They made their appearance about 2000 B.C.; some five hundred years later, as the result probably of a gradual process of infiltration and conquest, they had established that remarkable civilization which we know as Mycenaean, from the name of one of its most important sites, Mycenae, *Mykenai,* which was also the first on the Greek mainland to be explored. This civilization was by no means the fruit solely of the enterprise of the newcomers and their subjugation of the native population. Like the Germanic invaders of the Roman Empire, they profited by the resources of an older culture already existing and, at least materially, far higher than their own.

On the island of Crete there existed a culture which we call Minoan, from Minos, the name or title of a legendary king of that island. These Minoans, of unknown origin and speech, had established a strong government, the head of which was a king who possibly claimed actual divinity and not merely supreme human authority. They were enterprising seafarers, trading with a great part of the then known world; they had relations of one sort or another with the ancient kingdoms of the Near East and of Egypt; they had an elaborate system of writing, apparently hieroglyphic like the Egyptian; and they developed both the fine and the useful arts to an astonishing degree. The Achaians came to know this civilization, and ultimately destroyed it, for they were ruthless and enterprising fighters, comparatively well organized for war, and they became seafarers, by sheer force of circumstances it would seem. The ultimate result was a serious economic and social setback for the eastern Mediterranean, now no longer policed by the Minoan fleets nor kept clear of pirates, and with its network of trade relations broken; but in the meantime the Achaians raised their own standard of living markedly, using the services of Minoan craftsmen to make them all manner of fine things which they themselves had not the skill to produce. Ultimately their organization broke down, partly at least as the result of a series of wars against foreigners and among themselves, of which the sagas of Thebes and Troy (see Chapter III) are reflections, and there followed the much poorer age known as sub-Mycenaean which, together with the invasion of the Dorians, a more backward branch of the same stock as the

Achaians, brought at least the material culture of Greece to a low ebb, from which it had slowly and painfully to climb during the Archaic period (eighth to sixth centuries B.C.) to attain the glories of the full classical epoch. We catch an echo of the sub-Mycenaean epoch and its regrets for past splendours in Homer, who continually tells us that this or that feat of his heroes would not be possible for 'mortals such as now are'.

But from the Mycenaean epoch there remained a considerable legacy. The exploits of their warlike kings and nobles, however disastrous economically, form the material of every important group of sagas that has come down to us, for there is none which is not associated with a site known to have been Mycenaean. These tales were passed on largely by professional poets, reciters of heroic ballads, whose art gradually developed into the full-blown epic of which Homer is the supreme example. At what date any of the resulting poems were first written down we cannot say, but it has of late been made at least highly probable that the Achaians adopted one of the simpler forms of Minoan writing and used it as best they might for records couched in their speech, which was an early form of the Greek tongue. Later this was forgotten, for the classical Greeks took over and adapted the infinitely more convenient North Semitic alphabet, the foundation also of our own system of writing; but its use, however temporary and however limited, may have contributed to the concept of literature as being what the name implies, something which is written down and so preserved for posterity, independent of fallible human memory.

The Achaians thus told stories, and it is both improbable in itself and contradicted by some evidence that these stories dealt only with the warlike or other doings of their own ancestors. More than one traditional tale is related to the mythologies of the Near East. Several deal with the adventures of personages whose names show them to be no Achaians but members of the pre-Achaian population, the Helladics. Some have their scene laid in Crete, and it is far from impossible that here and there they preserve some fragment of the products of Minoan imagination, doubtless more or less garbled in transmission. Their successors therefore, the Greeks of the Archaic and Classical periods, inherited a stock of legends of

13

varied origin, as their own origin was mixed, partly Achaian, partly pre-Achaian.

We must now ask of what kind these traditional tales were, and a little inspection shows us that they fall into three classes, myths proper, sagas and *märchen,* or folktales. A myth is the result of imaginative reflection, the precursor we may say of scientific curiosity and hypotheses, on striking natural phenomena and still more on the religious beliefs and practices of the people. For instance: why does the sun appear to cross the sky daily from east to west ? The Greek picture of the process was that of a charioteer driving a marvellous team of shining horses across the sky, conceived as a solid vault over-arching the approximately flat earth. How the sun got back again without being seen was a subsidiary question variously answered; one explanation was that he sailed in a huge cup along the great river Okeanos (whence our 'ocean') that was supposed to encircle the earth. Or again: why do the Eleusinians and later the Athenians at Eleusis perform yearly the famous rites of the Mysteries, at which Kore, the corn-maiden, is carried off and sundry other strange things are done in some kind of ceremonial dance or semi-dramatic performance ? Answer, because Hades-Pluton, lord of the underworld, wanted a wife and so kidnapped Kore, who now is allowed to revisit her mother Demeter in the upper world every year, spending part of the time with her and part of it with her husband. Here we have the myth, embodied in the hymn to Demeter which used to be ascribed to Homer, side by side with what we can guess concerning the secret ritual. In some peoples a myth of this sort, what the Greeks called a *hieròs lógos* or holy story, is itself an important part of ritual, being recited ceremonially and only at certain times of the year and at certain hours of the day or night, and the supposed effect of such a recital is to maintain things as they are and have been since they were established by the supernatural beings long ago; for instance, to make the corn continue to grow and ripen every year, to keep the present orderly world in being and not revert to primaeval conditions in which, it may be, there was no sun and the earth was always dark, or the like, or to preserve the social organization of the people to whom the myth belongs. Evidence, however, that Greek myths were ever used in this way is lacking, and they remain a kind of imaginative commentary on the natural phenomena the Greeks observed and on their own customs, especially religious. They certainly never took the place of a creed, for Greek religion was creedless, a matter of doing certain things in the traditional manner, supposed to be agreeable to the gods concerned, and not of believing this or that. It is indeed very likely that the majority of Greeks, especially in early times, believed their myths to be true, but there was nothing to hinder or penalize those who found them incredible or tried to explain them away as allegories or misunderstandings. Impiety, *asebeia,* which was a punishable offence at Athens for instance, was essentially neglect of ritual or occasionally the publication of theories which denied the existence of some or all deities and thus did away with the basic reason for worshipping them at all.

Of very different origin were those narratives which are variously known as sagas (saga is simply the Scandinavian word for a story) or legends (a term which I prefer to use in a more general sense, to signify any traditional tale). These, however full of fictitious detail, have a historical basis, and represent either the popular memory or some imaginative writer's colouring of a real happening which was remarkable enough to be remembered more or less correctly. To this class belong, as already mentioned in passing, the tales of the wars of the Seven and their sons against Thebes, the long and complicated tale of Troy and the blood-stained history of the family of Pelops. That Thebes really did fall in an early war, that Troy was besieged and taken by someone, are assured facts, and that the dynasty to which Agamemnon belonged was troubled by bitter family quarrels resulting in murders of kinsman by kinsman is a thing in no way impossible nor even improbable. But we need not for that reason believe, for instance, that various gods took part in the attack and defence of Troy nor that Atreus caused his brother Thyestes to eat the flesh of his own sons. How active the popular mind continued to be in adding picturesque details to facts and in distorting the facts themselves we may see if we examine the historical excursuses in the Attic orators and compare what they say with the sober accounts preserved in such writers as Thucydides. But we have only to remember the ballad of Chevy Chase to understand that an excellent story may be the offspring of badly distorted history.

Finally come those tales, comparatively few in Greece, which are usually known as *märchen,* a convenient German word taken over into other languages. 'Fairy-tale' is quite inappropriate and misleading, for such stories need not deal with fairies or other supernatural beings, nor indeed with incredible events or persons. They are what the late Canon J. A. MacCulloch happily styled the childhood of fiction, the product of unknown authors, and they pass from mouth to mouth, indeed from people to people, crossing barriers of language, so that we find, for example, the tale of the one-eyed giant in Homer, who had it we may suppose from some popular tradition, and in Lapland. Hence they are not inappropriately called folktales. They differ from myths and sagas in that they originated simply in a desire to amuse. Perhaps the most remarkable feature of them is the similarity of certain events in them, what are technically known as motifs, in widely different parts of the world. For instance, no one is surprised to find in any story from anywhere an incident in which someone, fleeing from a formidable enemy (wizard, ogre or the like) delays his pursuer by throwing behind him objects, generally magical, which hinder the pursuit. The study of these motifs has in modern times been scientific and thorough, and anyone who is even slightly acquainted with the results of this research can recognize a *märchen* even when disguised, as it may come to be, as part of a myth or a saga. Failure to recognize such a tale for what it is has in the past led to strange misinterpretations and gross misunderstandings of the customs and beliefs of peoples and of their historical traditions.

In any given narrative, and not least in those of ancient Greece, all the above kinds of story may be blended, especially if the tale is long and elaborate and still more especially, perhaps, if it is old enough to have been many times retold. Thus the Troy-saga is ultimately based on a real war between Achaians of Greece proper with some of the islands and an apparently kindred Power established in Asia Minor. So far, then, it is saga. But it is often concerned with the doings of gods, and that is rather myth, and here and there an episode is to be found which is pure *märchen.* Nevertheless, it is necessary to bear in mind the different nature of these forms of legend, or else we shall be in danger of falling into some of the many absurdities committed by interpreters, ancient and modern, of traditional tales.

In the next three chapters stories will be dealt with according to their principal characteristics, myths in one chapter, sagas in another, *märchen* in the third, but attention will be drawn from time to time to features belonging to tales of a different kind which have crept in. Elaborate and detailed analysis is not possible in a book of this size, and those who wish for it are referred to the larger works mentioned in the bibliography, and to the many studies of separate points of interest to which they in turn refer.

II

THE MYTHS

Since Greek myths are largely concerned with the doings of gods, indeed several of them may be called biographies of deities, it is well to begin by knowing the names and traditional relationships of the principal objects of worship, together with those of a few figures whom any Greek of classical times would allow to be divine, but who never, so far as can be discovered, had any sort of cult in Greece.

According to the account given in Hesiod (probably eighth century B.C.), and before him implicit to a large extent in Homer, in the beginning was Chaos, 'the Void', from which sprang Earth (Gaia, Ge or Ga in various dialects of Greek). She in turn produced Uranos, personified Heaven, and they mated. This, the union of Father Sky and Mother Earth, is one of the most widespread of mythical themes, and reappears in sundry forms, especially in the complicated relationships of Zeus to females both mortal and immortal. This primal cosmic pair had numerous offspring, besides the children which Earth produced without consort. The latter included Night, who in turn became the mother of Day, and Pontos, personified Sea. But to Earth and her husband were born a group of deities collectively known as the Titans, the chief of whom was Kronos, who wedded his sister Rhea. These Titans, instigated by their mother, rebelled against Uranos, for so long as he and Earth remained embraced there was no room between them, and the children were hidden in caves and hollows. Gaia armed Kronos with a toothed sword or sickle, obviously the flint-studded reaping-hook of early days before metal sickles were in use. He succeeded in castrating his father, and from the blood of the mutilation Gaia was once more fertilized, the offspring including the Erinyes, or powers who avenge wrong done to one's kin, the Giants

19

and the Meliai, nymphs of manna-ashes, of whom more will be said later. The severed member itself fell into the sea, and from the foam, *aphros,* which gathered around it sprang Aphrodite, goddess of love, marriage and beauty, who at once made her way to Cyprus, the seat of her oldest cult in the Greek world. That is Hesiod's story, but more commonly Aphrodite is a daughter of Zeus by his consort Dione. Similarly, to Hesiod Eros (Love, actually a minor deity having a local cult at Thespiai in Boiotia) is one of the primal powers, child of Earth without consort; usually, he is the son of Aphrodite. In other words, Hesiod is a systematizer, already beginning to feel his way towards those concepts of cosmic forces which were later to occupy the attention of early philosophers, and consequently we must often discount what he says if we are to arrive at the genuinely popular myth.

Kronos was now lord of the universe, and took precautions against being overthrown in his turn by a family rebellion. He seems to have had no fear of his daughters, Hestia the hearth-goddess, Demeter the corn-goddess, and Hera, whose chief concern was the life of women; but as each of his sons, Hades, Poseidon and Zeus, was born, he swallowed the baby, who being immortal survived this harsh treatment. Zeus, however, escaped it by the contrivance of Rhea, who substituted a stone wrapped in swaddling-clothes for the infant and sent him away (it is generally said to Crete, which had a cult of a child-god identified with Zeus by the Greeks) to be brought up secretly. He was given milk by the goat (or nymph) Amaltheia and attended by the Kuretes, who smothered his cries by dancing war-dances about him and clashing their swords and shields—a piece of genuine Cretan ritual executed it would seem by the young men, *kouroi,* in honour of their young god. On attaining maturity, Zeus rose in rebellion against his father, who by Gaia's contrivance had vomited up the other sons and also the stone, which in later ages was venerated at Delphoi; in other words, the holiness of an ancient rude stone monument of some kind was explained by bringing it into contact with this strange myth, which has hardly a parallel in Greek (see below, p. 25) and may well be of foreign origin, whether Oriental or pre-Greek. There ensued now a war between Kronos and the Titans on the one hand, Zeus and his brothers on the other.

The latter were aided by sundry ancient powers, Kottos, Briareos and Gyes, of enormous size and strength, children of Uranos, whom Kronos had imprisoned in the depths of the earth and Zeus now released. They not only fought for him but gave him his typical weapons, thunder and lightning. Kronos and his party were thus overcome and in their turn imprisoned in Tartaros, the dungeon beneath the earth; though several later versions give Kronos himself a milder fate, exile to somewhere far in the west, accounts of his abode varying from an island off Great Britain to one of the terrestrial paradises of which we shall have to speak later (p. 30), and including Italy, where he became identified with the local god Saturnus.

The story of Zeus now continues with two main features, his dealings with mankind and his unions with goddesses and mortal women. But before settling peacefully as lord of the universe, he had at least one further struggle, in some accounts more than one. Earth bore one more child, the many-headed and many-handed monster Typhon or Typhoeus, who is perhaps a personification of storms. At all events he attacked the gods, and in one version of the story, preserved in late writers only, but so strange and grotesque that it seems both early and foreign, he managed to get possession of Zeus' sword and with it disabled him by cutting out the sinews of his arms and legs. Sword and sinews alike were recovered by a trick (the tricksters, as we have the story, were Hermes, see p. 50, and Pan, see p. 32, or Kadmos, see p. 85). Zeus, with his strength restored and his weapon given him again, re-engaged the monster and utterly overcame him; or, especially in accounts which omit this strange episode, he destroyed him with his thunderbolts and buried him under Mt Etna, which has belched flames ever since. But there is another contest, not to be found earlier than the sixth century B.C. in either art or literature; Hesiod for instance has never heard of it. Earth brought forth a whole brood of giants who assailed the gods. These called Herakles to their aid (see pp. 112 f.) and with this formidable human ally they overcame their enormous and, as oftenest represented or described, monstrous foes. The tale is pretty certainly derived from one of the Oriental creation-myths in which a god or gods defeats some primaeval monster, for instance the Babylonian Marduk

21

overcomes Tiamat. But when the Greeks adopted it, it is
simply an episode in the history of the divine dynasty, so to
call it. Greek gods do not create the world, though they
sometimes make or discover some feature of it.

Zeus' relations with his own family were, if not entirely
harmonious, not so unfriendly as seriously to imperil his
position as head of it. Homer does indeed mention a plot of
Hera, Poseidon and Athene to bind, and so presumably
depose, him which was foiled by the minor sea-goddess Thetis
calling Briareos to his assistance, but this is an isolated story
belonging to some tradition now lost (we must remember that
Homer, our earliest authority, is on any possible dating a
millennium or so later than the first arrival of the Achaians in
Greece, and doubtless many myths have never been recorded
because he has no occasion to mention them). Zeus' brothers
assented peacefully enough to his superior position. Perhaps
the commonest story is that after their victory they cast lots
and Zeus got heaven, Poseidon the sea and Hades the underworld, earth remaining their common property and Olympos,
or the sky, their common dwelling; Olympos being in this case
a lofty mountain in Thessaly, the top of which, to the rudi-
mentary cosmography of those days, would easily be thought
to touch the sky and be a sort of vestibule of it, wherefore it
remains throughout classical times the traditional dwelling-
place of the celestial gods. In most accounts also, including
Homer's, Zeus is not the youngest brother, as in Hesiod, but
the eldest, and although the Greeks had no law of primo-
geniture, that would give him a position of some superiority.

Mankind was not the creation of Zeus, but existed before
he came into power; as already mentioned, Greek deities are
not creators in any proper sense. In this connexion we meet
with a curious and interesting figure, to be paralleled, however, from the folklore and traditions of other peoples. This is
Prometheus, the Foreseer, that is to say the provident, crafty
person who, like similar figures elsewhere, is not always on
good terms with the chief god but on occasion is too clever
for him. There is a tradition, preserved in no very ancient
author (mentions of it are to be found in Horace, in Pausanias'
guidebook to Greece, written in the second century A.D., and
in some minor writers), that he actually made man, shaping
our earliest ancestors out of clay. That this is really a popular

tradition is fairly well proved by the existence at Panopeus, a town of Phokis in central Greece, of some lumps of clay which were shown to visitors as being left over from Prometheus' work. In proof of their statement, the natives drew attention to the smell of this clay, which they claimed resembled that of the human body. At all events, Prometheus appears on occasion as the champion of mankind against Zeus himself. There is an amusing and obviously old myth explaining why at sacrifices only the less edible portions of the victim, especially the entrails, are offered to the gods, while the bones are usually buried on consecrated ground. Men and gods, it seems, met to discuss the proper division of sacrificial animals, and Prometheus made two bundles, one containing the bones and so forth of an ox, covered with fat, while the other contained the best of the meat, closely covered with hide, and gave Zeus his choice. The god chose the attractive-looking fat (Hesiod, who is our authority, is so concerned for the divine wisdom that he spoils the story by making Zeus only pretend to be deceived), and ever since then, man has used the best parts of the victim for his share of the sacrificial banquet. Zeus was very angry, and devised two punishments for man. First he prevented firesticks from producing any fire, but Prometheus stole fresh fire, apparently from heaven, and brought it to earth in a stalk of giant fennel, the pith of which will smoulder a long while and so was used for such a purpose. Then he had Hephaistos fashion a woman, whom Athene and Aphrodite made extremely attractive. She was the first of all women, the ancestress of female kind, and Prometheus' stupid brother Epimetheus (Afterthinker, i.e., wise after the event) welcomed her, though Prometheus had warned him not to accept any present from Zeus. The woman, whose name was Pandora (interpreted by the ancients as All-gifted, because the gods bestowed all manner of gifts, such as beauty, on her; it really means All-giver, and she probably is an old earth-goddess), opened a store-jar in which were contained all sorts of diseases and other evils, and let them loose to plague mankind; the jar remained empty but for hope, which was caught under the lid when it was closed again.

Prometheus, in the authors we have, was exalted far above the position of trickster or master-thief which he seems originally to have occupied, and held also a respectable place in cult, being worshipped by craftsmen here and there because of his connexion with fire. In Aeschylus' *Prometheus Bound* he is the unselfish champion and rescuer of mankind, to whom he gave not only fire but instruction in all useful arts, and is the victim of relentless persecution by Zeus, who binds him to a rock on a mountain-top and sends his eagle to tear his liver. Prometheus, however, holds a secret which he will not divulge, namely that the sea-goddess Thetis is destined to bear a son mightier than his father, and consequently if Zeus or Poseidon marries her, as both were anxious to do, her child will overthrow the divine dynasty. Ultimately a compromise was reached and Prometheus set free, but the loss of Aeschylus' second play on the subject prevents us from knowing the details, and especially how he reconciled his own lofty view of Zeus as the righteous ruler of the world with his cruelty to Prometheus. The latter, by the way, has already in Hesiod a respectable genealogy, being a son of the Titan Iapetos.

By general consent, life became harder for man under Zeus. In Kronos' time there was the Golden Age, in which there was no need to work, because the earth untilled brought forth all that man wanted. Since then it has not been so. Hesiod lists five successive ages, the Golden, the Silver, the Bronze, the Heroic and the present, or Iron Age. Each was worse than the one before it, except that the age of the heroes (approximately the Mycenaean period) was an improvement on the preceding, and the men of that time, having valiantly perished in war, were transported to the Islands of the Blessed, where the land bears them three crops a year and they live a carefree life. The Iron Age holds no hope, but will grow steadily worse.

Man presently degenerated to the extent of becoming intolerably sinful, and Zeus was provoked to destroy humankind by a flood. But, as in the Semitic flood-legends, there was a righteous man, Deukalion, who with his wife Pyrrha was warned by Prometheus his father to take refuge in a boat. When the flood receded, they were divinely advised to throw the bones of their mother, which they correctly interpreted as the stones of the earth. When they did so, those thrown by Deukalion became men and those thrown by Pyrrha women, and so man was re-created. Incidentally, this explains why the Greek word for 'people' is *laos*; it comes (according to ancient etymologists) from *laas, a* stone.

As to the marriages of Zeus, his original consort was probably Dione, whose name is a feminine form of his own (see p. 20), but his official wife is his sister Hera, who bore him Ares the war-god and Eileithyia, the birth-goddess, also Hebe, who is Youth personified. But from his own head Zeus produced Athena. Hesiod, by means of a patent allegory, explains this by saying that Zeus had wedded Metis (Wisdom or Good Counsel) and swallowed her when she was with child. In other words, the supreme god always has wisdom in him. Hera, by a counter-miracle, bore Hephaistos the fire-god and patron of smiths without father. Zeus also wedded Themis, who is probably to begin with simply Mother Earth once more (her name means something like 'firm, unmoved'), but develops into a goddess of justice. Her offspring were the Horai, who are not hours in our sense (that meaning of the word is much later) but the seasons of the year, and so vary in number according to how the seasons were reckoned. She also bore the Moirai, that is to say the Allotters, who seem originally to have been birth-goddesses who assigned to each newborn child his lot in life, as in modern Greek belief they still do, but developed into deities of destiny in general, commonly represented as spinning a thread which is the life and fate of men. Their names are Klotho, Lachesis and Atropos, that is to say Spinner, Lot-giver and Inflexible. A daughter of Okeanos (p. 14), Eurynome, bore the Charities (the Latin Gratiae or Graces), who, though they developed into goddesses of beauty or grace in our sense, were pretty certainly to begin with agricultural deities whose function it was to make tilled ground look 'winsome' or 'delightful' because bearing a good crop. His sister Demeter bore him Kore-Persephone, queen of the underworld by her marriage with Hades (see p. 14), while Mnemosyne (Memory) became the mother by him of the nine Muses (approximately 'Reminders'), Kleio, Euterpe, Thaleia, Melpomene, Terpsichore, Erato, Polymnia, Urania and Kalliope, who between them preside over all manner of arts and sciences, the assignment of each of them to some particular art being a fancy of late times and no part of their original nature. Leto the

Titaness bore Zeus twins, Apollo and Artemis, and by Maia, one of the Pleiads, daughters of the great Titan Atlas whose task it is to uphold the sky, he had Hermes. Semele daughter of Kadmos (see p. 85) became pregnant by him, but was advised by Hera, frantically jealous as always, to ask Zeus to appear to her in his true form. This was too much for mortal eyes to behold, and she perished amid the blaze of his thunderbolts, but he saved the unborn child, inserted him in his own thigh, and then produced him at full time. This was the god Dionysos. Evidence from other languages, including Phrygian, makes it clear that Semele is the name of no mortal woman, but (in the form Zemelo) a name of the Earth; hence we have once more the primal pair, Earth and Heaven.

Thus Greek instinct for systematization brought the chief gods and some who are of less importance into one great family. In point of fact, their origin is extremely varied. The only one whom we can be certain the Achaians brought into Greece with them was Zeus himself, whose name, as has long been recognized, is etymologically the same as the Sanskrit Dyaus and the first syllable of the Latin Iup-piter and therefore belongs to the original language, Indo-Germanic or Wiro, spoken before the users of it broke up into separate groups and carried varieties of their tongue into new areas. Hades is traditionally 'the Unseen One', *A-(w)ides,* which I still think the correct etymology, though another, which would connect it with *aia,* one of the forms of the word for 'earth', is now popular. Poseidon's name is of doubtful origin. Its oldest known form is Poseidaon, which has been ingeniously explained as 'oh husband of Da', Da being, it is suggested, an old name of the pre-Greek earth-goddess. Certainly this accords with his oldest known functions and his very ancient title Gaiaochos, 'holder (embracer) of Earth'. The Achaians to all appearance came from some inland region and did not know the sea till they arrived in Greece; and it is quite conceivable that they evolved an earth-god mated with a native goddess of the earth and its fertility. But the derivation is neither certain nor the only one that has been put forward. Demeter or Damater, according to dialect (classical Greek split into some ten dialects in all), is perhaps again a compound of the supposed name of the local earth-goddess with the pure Greek title Mater or Meter, 'mother', which would be appropriate for a deity whose chief functions are connected with the soil and the corncrop. Her daughter seems a combination of two different goddesses, Kore, 'the Maiden', that is the young corn of the new harvest, and Persephone (or Persephassa, with yet other variants of the plainly foreign name), queen of the underworld. Deities of the earth, generally known as chthonians, from *chthon,* an old name for earth, are really of two kinds, those who have to do with the surface of the ground and its fruits and those who govern the depths of the earth, where the dead go when their remains, burned or not, are buried; but the two classes tend to be confused in popular Greek thought. This is why Persephone's husband, HADES, is also called Pluton, which means 'wealthy', that is to say owner and presumably giver of the chief source of wealth to a people mainly agricultural, the fruits of the earth. He, like her, is a blend of two distinct deities. The real name of HERA, if she had a name, is unknown, for Hera seems to be the feminine of *heros,* the original meaning of which is a gentleman, a man of good family, and so signifies no more than 'lady'. She had a very ancient cult at Argos and elsewhere, and the Achaians, who like all polytheists were very tolerant of and respectful towards new deities, adopted her cult and thought of her as the consort of their own chief god, thus displacing Dione except at what is perhaps the oldest centre in Greece of the worship of Zeus, Dodona. ATHENA (ATHANA, ATHENE) undoubtedly is a native goddess of the pre-Achaian population. Her name has the suffix characteristic of the pre-Greek language, *-na-,* and means nothing in Greek. Her worship is associated with hills, and so she easily became the protectress of the strongholds of Mycenaean lords, and when their power had ceased to be, her temple replaced the old castle, as was assuredly the case at her most famous centre of cult, Athens (*Athenai*). ARTEMIS may also be a survival from pre-Achaian days and is quite likely to have been originally not the virgin she consistently is in classical tradition but a goddess of more maternal type. It has repeatedly been pointed out that nymphs associated with her are often said to have become mothers, and there is room for the supposition that at least some of them are no more than titles of the goddess made independent; for instance, Kallisto (see p. 48) has a name suspiciously like Artemis' title Kalliste (fairest). As to her name, a by-form of it in Doric is Artamis, and that suggests the noun *artamos,* a slaughterer, which agrees fairly well with her activity as a huntress, though to kill a beast with arrows and to butcher it are not the same thing. But whatever her origin, she was widely popular and worshipped under a variety of titles, though she was not, it would seem, originally a deity to whom the upper classes paid much attention. She is the goddess especially of the wilds, of country outside the limits of cultivation, and of all that live in it, and a patroness of hunters, which is why she is shown as a huntress herself; a bringer of sudden death to women yet at the same time their helper in childbirth and the protectress not of their offspring only but of all young things. In any case, she has no original connexion with the very different APOLLO, and why he is said to be her twin is a puzzle, unless the fact that both are archers has something to do with it. His name yields no convincing Greek etymology, though many attempts have been made to find one, and many indications, not wholly convincing yet not to be neglected, connect him with the Near East, where he may have originated. Many of his functions can be plausibly explained by supposing that he was originally what his title Nomios (He of the pastures) implies, a god of herdsmen. Anyone having charge of beasts in their summer pastures especially, that is to say on high ground where the grass stays green and edible far longer than on the plains, would need to be able to protect them against wolves and robbers, and his natural weapon would be the bow, such as Apollo regularly carries. He must also know something of the cure of hurts, theirs and his own and those of his companions, which might account for the god's medical activities. Further, it has been for many centuries a herdsman's custom to use a musical instrument both to call the cattle, who get to know a particular strain of music belonging to their own herd, and for his own amusement. This might well connect with the musical activities of Apollo, one of whose titles is Musagetes (Leader of the Muses), were it not that he is constantly shown as a lyre-player, while the pastoral instrument is the pipe. But none of these considerations tell us how he became a prophetic deity, inspiring his priestess at Delphoi by possession not unlike that of a Siberian shaman, nor how he developed into a specialist in purifications and the great authority on ritual law, constantly consulted as to the best method of conducting the worship of a State or the correct procedure for avoiding the evil consequences of some event supposedly portentous or getting rid of some visitation such as a plague. Perhaps his most outstanding feature is that whatever his origin he developed into the most characteristically Greek of all the gods, thought of as embodying in his person the highest type of manly beauty in young maturity and author of traditional maxims recommending typically Greek moderation and sobriety. It may be mentioned in passing that he has no solar features whatever, his identification with the Sun, Helios, who has no worship in Greece proper, being a theory which gained popularity from the fifth century B.C. onwards but is patently false.

Of the rest of Zeus' near kin, his sister Hestia has a good claim to have been originally an Achaian deity, though this is not certain. At all events, a goddess of the hearth is a highly probable object of the worship of any people which can build houses with fireplaces in them, and the similarity in sound between her name and that of the Roman Vesta may not be an accident. But she is quite unimportant for mythology, for she has practically no myths. Zeus' son HERMES, or HERMEIAS, is certainly an old god, worshipped originally, it would seem, in Arkadia, his traditional birthplace being Mt Kyllene. His name may be connected with *herma,* that is to say stone, with reference to the stone-heaps or cairns which in Greece as in many countries served to mark out tracks or primitive roads, perhaps also to indicate spots felt to be uncanny for some reason. It would be quite natural for 'him of the cairn' to emerge from such a custom, and to be accordingly honoured by the users of roads, namely merchants travelling to buy or sell, heralds going with messages from one community to another, and robbers who preyed on travellers, all of whom are under Hermes' protection. We do not know by what means he became also patron of young men and their activities, especially athletic, and so the patron of their *palaestrae* or wrestling-schools, and by a further development of their cultural studies, especially rhetoric and poetry. It is at all events in this connexion that he acquires his common symbol, the cock, which cannot have originally been his, for domestic poultry were not imported into Greece till comparatively late.

The allusion is to the popular sport of cock-fighting. He is himself shown in art as a handsome young man, perhaps some nineteen or twenty years old, wearing the *petasos* or broad-brimmed hat favoured by travellers and carrying a herald's staff, *kerykeion,* in Latin *caduceus.* He also on occasion carries a conjuror's wand, being one of the few Greek deities who have anything to do with magic.

With one exception, it is not clear if the Titans were ever gods of cult; the exception is KRONOS himself, whose name set ancient etymologists guessing, their most popular suggestion being that it is another form of Chronos, Time. This is doubly impossible, for formally, the aspirated palatal which we transliterate by *ch* does not lose its aspirate, and materially, Time is far too abstract a conception to be an object of really ancient cult, as apparently Kronos is. In Hekatombaion, the first month of the Attic year (roughly equivalent to July), came the Kronia, or festival of Kronos, one of those merry-makings which are perhaps especially characteristic of harvest-time (a season of course considerably earlier in a Mediterranean climate than in Great Britain and the rest of northern Europe). There was feasting, and during it masters and servants ate together. It is not uncommon to find seasonal feasts in various parts of the world at which ordinary social rules are set aside for the time being; the Romans noted with interest that the proceedings resembled their own Saturnalia, or festival of Saturnus, although this came in December, not in late summer. This is probably one of the reasons why they identified Saturnus with Kronos and thus gave rise to the story (see p. 164) that the exiled god found a new home in Italy. Loosely connected with the Titanic family as children either of Earth herself or of some of her numerous offspring are a few figures of some importance in mythology or in cult. Pontos for instance (see p. 19) had a son Nereus, probably an ancient sea-god displaced by Poseidon, who had a reputation for wisdom and truthfulness and became by his wife Doris the father of the Nereids, the mermaids of Greek tradition. Okeanos had a daughter Elektra (Shining One) who married Thaumas and bore him Iris, the personified rainbow, and the Harpies (*Harpyiai*), apparently wind-spirits, for their chief business in myth is to carry someone or something away, but in later tradition, from Alexandrian times down, we find them represented as bird-like creatures with the faces of women, insatiably greedy and exceedingly filthy and repulsive. Their name means 'snatchers'. Keto, another child of Pontos, had monstrous offspring, appropriately (*ketos* is a sea-monster), the Graiai, who are personified old age—the name means approximately 'old women'—of whom more will be said when telling the story of Perseus and the Gorgons, Sthenno, Euryale and Medusa, i.e., Strong One, Wide-leaping and Queen, of whom the last was mortal, and will also be heard of in the same context.

Finally, DIONYSOS according to nearly all our evidence was a late-comer into Greece and HEPHAISTOS, though somewhat earlier (for Homer is quite familiar with him and mentions Dionysos very little) is manifestly so. The former god seems to have become fully established in Greek cult hardly earlier than about the seventh century B.C. He apparently originated in Thrace, and was a god of the fertility and energy of nature. That he tended to specialize as a wine-god in Greece is probably due to the existence of older deities who were concerned with fertility, but if he had originally been such, his festivals would occur at times important for viticulture and wine-making, which they do not. His characteristic worship was wild, orgiastic dancing and running in the open air, on hilltops, not infrequent in winter, the result of which was so to excite the participants that they seemed to lose their own personality and be merged in that of their god, which is why they and he alike bear the title Bakchos (Bakchoi, Bakchai), whatever it may mean, and the female votaries are often called Mainades (Maenads), that is to say madwomen. This was all so unlike the normal orderly Greek worship that we may suppose some of the stories of the god's arrival (see pp. 52ff.) to reflect actual opposition to him and his cult. Hephaistos' progress can be traced by simply plotting on a map the position of his known shrines. They come thickest as we approach the volcanic region of Asia Minor, making it very probable that he was to begin with a deity of volcanic fires. The Greeks soon specialized him into a god of those who use fire, especially smiths, and he largely displaced Prometheus (see p. 23) in this capacity. Hence in Greece the evidence for his cult is most abundant in comparatively industrialized districts, such as Attica, and rare or absent in more backward places.

It would seem that the Greeks from about Homer's time onward, and probably from much earlier, had lost all clear consciousness of the very mixed origin of their deities, remembering only that Dionysos came from abroad or that Aphrodite was especially associated with Cyprus and not with the mainland. They were all members of one great family, the head of which, *patér* (a word which does not imply begetting but natural authority), was Zeus. Numerous minor powers, worshipped here and there in the country, were not included, at least normally, in any such genealogy, and if they had any myths they have not come down to us, wherefore they need not be considered in a book of this kind. Others were 'faded' to use a modern technicality, being thought of as mortals somehow associated with gods, generally as heroes, that is to say venerable ghosts powerful at least in the neighbourhood of their tombs. One godling gained a certain importance, though not a fixed genealogy (he is sometimes son of Hermes). That is PAN (Feeder, Pasturer) an Arkadian god of herdsmen. He has but few myths, tales about him being mostly accounts of how he appeared to this or that mortal or struck 'panic' terror into someone. His shape is always more or less goatish, the most characteristic representations in art and literature portraying him as partly human but with the legs, horns and beard of a he-goat. Also loosely attached and sometimes associated with one of the greater deities are the spirits of the wild, if 'spirits' is not too etherial a name for them, the SATYRS and SEILENOI and the NYMPHS. Satyrs (*Satyroi*; the etymology is highly uncertain) are thought of as more or less misshapen little men (Attic art gave them horses' tails), extremely lustful and full of mischief. The Seilenoi, or in the singular Seilenos, are, or is, an elder and slightly more sober kind of Satyr, often represented as their leader. Nymphs (the word *nymphai* means young marriageable women or brides) are fairy-like beings supposed to haunt various natural features such as forests, springs, rivers and so forth, wherefore they are often distinguished by adjectival names, as Dryads (*dryades,* from *drys,* a tree or specifically an oak) and Hamadryads, who haunt trees, the latter especially being sometimes the spirits of trees who die when the tree does, Naiads or spring-nymphs (*naein* means 'to flow'), Oreads, nymphs of the hills (*oros* is a hill or mountain), Potamiads, of rivers (*potamoi*) and so forth, though the classes are often confused. It was not an uncommon belief that Nymphs generally were very long-lived, but not immortal. Belief in them was lively, their little rustic shrines were familiar objects, and under the name of Neraidhes, i.e., Nereids, daughters of Nereus, they still have their place in modern folklore. The stories concerning them are not very numerous; they will be mentioned here and there in this book. They are often associated with Artemis, who indeed is now and then pluralized herself (*Artemides*); the Satyrs and Seilenoi are constantly shown as followers of Dionysos, who seems to have absorbed into his vigorous personality numerous little powers of fertility locally worshipped.

To tell all the myths in which ZEUS appears would be endless, for he is constantly represented as interfering in one way or another with the affairs of the lesser gods and of mankind. His amours are very numerous, for he is patterned on a great Mycenaean or sub-Mycenaean chieftain, who was monogamous but allowed by general consent to have relations with women other than his wife, usually women of inferior position and most often captives from his own wars or slaves bought from kidnappers. These women were in no way outcasts, nor were their children (*nothoi*). A *nothos* had indeed a recognized position in his father's family, although inferior to that of the legitimate sons. Hence if a god bestowed his favours upon a mortal woman, she suffered no dishonour but rather the opposite, and her child stood an excellent chance of becoming a prominent *heros*. It may well be that the stories we have of distinguished men begotten by gods (or, much less often, born of goddesses to mortal fathers) are the leavings of a much larger number, genealogical legends of families more or less prominent, like that of Hekataios of Miletos, who, Herodotos tells us, could trace his ancestry for fifteen human generations, the sixteenth being a god. They, and the affairs of gods with mortal women which are their starting-point, will be handled in the next chapter. The biography, so to call it of Zeus, is practically over when he becomes supreme god, for as he is immortal, it cannot go on to tell of his old age and death.

Concerning his brothers, there is not very much to tell. POSEIDON seems from the first to have been associated with horses as well as with the earth and its waters. It was in horse-shape that he loved and mated with Demeter at Thelpusa in Arkadia, and their offspring was Arion or Areion, not the poet but a wonderful horse, which came into possession of Adrastos (see p. 120). In his contest with Athena for the land of Attica he created a horse, she an olive-tree (cf. p. 37), and another of his loves was Medusa the Gorgon (see p. 31), from whose headless body after her death sprang the winged horse Pegasos. His hatred for Odysseus and the reasons for it will be dealt with in Chapter IV. His sons tended to be violent, like their father; the best known of them was Antaios the giant, Poseidon's son by Earth, whom we shall meet again in dealing with Herakles. Poseidon's legitimate consort is AMPHITRITE, a pale and unimportant being who seems to be an old sea-goddess; the syllable *trit-* occurs in several non-Greek names having to do with water. Their only child of the least importance is TRITON, the Greek merman, who is now one, now many, as often happens to such vague minor figures. He appears in a few obscure stories as a dangerous creature, easily provoked.

Of HADES there is little to say except his carrying off of KORE-PERSEPHONE, already mentioned (p. 14). In one of the best-known forms of the tale, found in the 'Homeric' hymn to Demeter, which is of about the seventh century B.C., she was picking flowers when he beguiled her by making an extraordinarily fine narcissus spring up. When she touched it, the earth gaped and he came up in his chariot and took her away. Demeter wandered far and wide looking for her daughter, and learned first from Hekate (a goddess originally Karian, of functions something like those of Artemis, with whom she is often confused; she later became the disreputable patroness of witches) and then from Helios (the Sun) that Hades had taken her by the connivance of Zeus. Therupon in great wrath she took the shape of an old woman and wandered about the earth, shunning the society of the gods, till she came to Eleusis, where she got a kindly reception from the household of its king Keleos and was employed as nurse to his child. In return for this she intended to make the baby immortal, the process being to rub him over with ambrosia (see p. 62) and lay him in the fire every night. But Metaneira, the child's mother, spied her one night and screamed in terror, whereat

Demeter took him out of the fire and revealed herself in her true form. But although the child thus remained mortal, Demeter still was gracious to the Eleusinians and taught them her rites. Meanwhile, with the corn-goddess absent, the crops were failing everywhere and the earth threatened with famine; Zeus therefore sought a reconciliation and it was agreed that Persephone should be returned to her mother. But Hades had induced her to eat some seeds of a pomegranate which he had handled, and this bound her to him at least to the extent of spending a third part of every year with him underground.

With this tale also we have practically exhausted the mythology of DÉMETER. That, as Homer and a few others mention, she lay with one Iasion or Iasios in a ploughed field probably goes back to some ancient rite intended to promote the growth of the crops. One or two legends set forth the terrible nature of her anger; the best known is the punishment of Erysichthon, a Thessalian prince who scorned her advice to spare a sacred grove from which he wanted to cut timber. She sent an insatiable hunger upon him, and he and his father's house were reduced to beggary.

HERA, important though she is, has not many myths of her own, though she appears as a character in story after story, sometimes as the jealous wife of Zeus, persecuting his numerous mistresses and their offspring, sometimes in what might be called her political aspect, favouring one city against another (in particular, she is the bitter enemy of Troy), now and then as favouring a particular hero, notably Jason (see p. 123). She is, as already mentioned, a goddess of women especially, which is why she was worshipped at Stymphalos in Arkadia as Pais, Teleia and Chera, that is to say Maid, Wife and Widow. These titles have nothing to do with her own characteristics but reflect the condition of the various classes of women who sought her help, a not infrequent origin of cult-titles of deities in both Greece and Rome, but puzzling to researchers ancient and modern until the true reason is seen. One of her most notable rites was the sacred marriage, *hieròs gámos*, in which the union of a god and goddess is solemnly celebrated with appropriate rites, such as a wedding-procession. It is not always certain by any means that the parties to the divine marriage were always Zeus and Hera, indeed it is likely enough that so celebrated a pair of deities often displaced others less known and perhaps nameless; but the following legends distinctly name them. The Boiotians had a tale that Hera was reared on the neighbouring island of Euboia, and that she and Zeus eloped together to Mt Kithairon, not far from Thebes. There Makris, the nymph of the island, who was Hera's duenna, came to look for her, but Kithairon, i.e., the supernatural power inhabiting the mountain, told her to go away, because Zeus was private with Leto the Titaness. Hence Hera and Leto were worshipped together locally, even identified, in sharp contrast to their usual relationship (see p. 40). In one or the other of the same sites Zeus won Hera back after a quarrel by a trick. Giving out that he was going to marry again, Zeus organized a wedding procession, with a dressed-up log of wood for the bride. Hera was furious, interrupted the procession, stripped the supposed bride and discovered that she was nothing but wood, and had enough sense of humour to laugh at the jest and be reconciled. This is an example of what we call an aetiological myth, that is one which gives the reason, *aition* in Greek, for some traditional performance. At intervals the Boiotians used to make wooden images from a tree chosen by divination, and every sixty years these images were solemnly burned on the top of Kithairon, after sacrifice to Zeus and Hera. Fortunately, it is not necessary in a book on mythology to go into the obscure question of what the ceremony actually meant to those who first established it. A few more legends related to particular statues of the goddess. One was at Samos, a very old seat of her cult. It used every year to be brought out of its temple, hidden under withies, and formally searched for, and the people explained that Tyrrhenian, that is to say Etruscan, pirates had once stolen it and were miraculously prevented from bringing it any farther. At Hermione in the Peloponnesos, the statue carried a sceptre on which was a cuckoo. This was explained as being Zeus himself, who had taken that form to make his amorous approaches to her, and it is possible that the bird was indeed divine, since Minoan deities seem often to have assumed birdshape. If so, it does not follow that it was originally Zeus, nor is it very likely.

ATHENA (ATHANA, ATHENE, ATHENAIE) has a rich store of myths, perhaps due at least in part to her position as tutelary goddess of the quick-witted and inventive Athenians, whose city is named after her, but partly also to her complex nature, for she is on the one hand a warlike goddess, generally shown in the armour of a Greek infantryman (*hoplites*) and on the other the patroness of all manner of arts and crafts (one of her titles is Ergane, 'working-woman'). To begin with, we have the story of how she came to be goddess of Athens and of Attica generally. As already mentioned, Poseidon was her rival, and to show his power he struck the rock of the Akropolis (the citadel of Athens) with the trident which is his characteristic attribute, generally interpreted as a fish-spear, though this is not certain. The marks are still to be seen under a porch of Athena's oldest temple, the Erechtheion (home of Erechtheus, cf. p. 80; it is visited by her in the *Odyssey*. A salt spring resulted, or a horse appeared; the latter is, as we have it, the later story, but there is nothing to prove that it does not go back to early times. Athena in her turn produced an olive-tree, the first of the sacred olives of Attica, which when burned by the Persians in 480 B.C. grew again at a miraculous rate. The judges, whether gods, the king of Athens or a jury of his people, pronounced her the victor, then Poseidon in anger flooded the Thriasian Plain, but was finally reconciled to Athena and her land. This much fact at least underlies the myth, that Poseidon was much honoured in Athens, being an aristocratic god with whom even the writers of Old Comedy, accustomed to making sport of deities, dealt with some respect.

Athena is regularly a virgin, which is what her very common title Pallas is generally supposed to mean. However, it is possible that like so many prehistoric goddesses of the Mediterranean region she was originally maternal, and possible also that the following legend is a faint reminiscence of this. Hephaistos wished to marry her and tried to overcome her by force. As they struggled his seed fell on the ground, which was thus fertilized and produced a child, Erichthonios, of whom Athena took charge. She put him in a chest and entrusted it to the daughters of Kekrops (see p. 80), forbidding them to open it, but their curiosity overcame them, and something that they saw inside drove them mad with fright, so that they leaped from the Akropolis and were killed. However, the earliest surviving accounts of Erichthonios, who seems to be originally

37

a minor god, say nothing of Hephaistos' part in the affair and too much should not be made of such uncertain evidence.

Her birth has already been mentioned (p. 25); sundry details are added and one or two fresh legends attached to it by authors later than Hesiod, and it is not always easy to say how much is genuine myth and how much due to their poetical imagination. The delivery of Zeus was accomplished by one of the more ingenious gods, but most often by Hephaistos, who split Zeus' skull with an axe and so let Athena out. An immortal god naturally would feel comparitively little inconvenience from this heroic midwifery. The Rhodians had a legend of their own, the aetiological myth of a local deity whom they identified with Athena; she had a temple in the town of Lindos. The Sun, to whom the island belonged, warned his sons of the coming birth and bade them be ready with sacrifice so as to be the first to do Athena honour. They obeyed, but in their haste forgot to bring any fire to the place of sacrifice, hence Athena of Lindos was worshipped with fireless offerings, i.e., her portion of the sacrificial victims was not burned. As this is characteristic of the worship of chthonian deities, it is fairly plain proof that the Lindian goddess was of that kind and therefore wrongly identified with Athena. Identifications of one divinity with another were common, however, in the ancient world and often made on the flimsiest grounds of chance resemblance.

Ingenious and a helper of the ingenious, Athena was credited with having invented various implements, one of them being the flute, or rather oboe, *aulos*, for it was a reed instrument played by blowing directly into, not across, the mouthpiece. Two legends attach themselves to this invention. One, the older as far as we know, is that she used it to imitate the wailings of the other two Gorgons when Medusa was killed (see p. 102) and the hissing of their snaky hair. The other is that she found blowing into it distorted her face unbecomingly and therefore she threw it away. It was picked up by Marsyas the Satyr, who soon became so expert in its use that he challenged Apollo to a musical contest, the winner to do what he liked with the loser. Apollo won and flayed Marsyas alive.

Athena possibly was not always virgin; APHRODITE has nothing virginal about her, but is a typical Oriental mother-goddess, though there is no agreement as to who her children are; Eros, so regularly her son in the later literature and art, has no early connexion with her in cult. The most obviously Eastern of her myths is that of her love for Adonis, whose name is the Semitic *adon* ('lord') and who is often identified with Ishtar's lover Tammuz. Whether this is right or wrong Adonis is of the same type as Tammuz, a consort of a mother-goddess who embodies the growth and withering of vegetation. His mother was a certain Myrrha or Smyrna, daughter of Theias king of Assyria or Kinyras king of Cyprus, who conceived a passion for her own father and contrived under cover of darkness to satisfy it. When he tried to kill her on finding out the truth, she prayed for deliverance and was turned into the balsam-tree which still bears her name. From the tree Adonis was born, and when he grew older he became a huntsman. Aphrodite saw him and loved him for his great beauty, but he was killed by a boar; different versions of the tale represent him as an ordinary animal of his kind, or as sent by Artemis, whose anger Adonis had somehow incurred, or even as being Ares in disguise, who was jealous of the young man. Sundry flowers sprang up from his blood, or from the tears Aphrodite shed for him, or owe their colour (the red of red roses) to Aphrodite's own blood, when she ran to help Adonis and was pricked by thorns. There is a totally different version, in which Aphrodite put the baby Adonis into a chest and entrusted him to Persephone, who was so struck by his beauty that she would not give him back until Zeus, mediating between the goddesses decreed that he should spend a third of the year with each and the remaining third where he chose.

Another lover of Aphrodite was Anchises of Troy, a prince of the junior branch of the royal house. He was very handsome when a young man, and either of her own whim or because Zeus sent the desire on her because she had caused him and the other gods so much trouble, she mated with him and bore Aineias, the Aeneas of Latin and modern tradition. This sounds like a real local tradition, not a piece of Greek poetic fancy; the Trojan dynasty had a cult of the Great Mother, who seems to have been worshipped on Mt Ida, near the city, and naturally claimed her as an ancestress, or at all events the clan of Aineias did so.

Coming to Greece, Aphrodite must to some extent at least

fall in with Greek ideas. Her cult was generally decent enough; it is quite the exception that at Corinth, a trading town and therefore open to foreign influences, she had temple-harlots, Oriental fashion. So also her personal conduct is somewhat toned down and she appears from Homer onwards (or at least from some early interpolator of the *Odyssey*) as a wife, her consort being another Oriental immigrant, Hephaistos. But for some reason which escapes us, she is sometimes connected with Ares in cult, and he appears as Hephaistos' dangerous rival. In the merry tale which Demodokos the minstrel sings for the Phaiakians to dance to (see p. 145), Hephaistos lays a trap for her and her lover in the shape of a net so fine as to be invisible but so strong as to be unbreakable. In this they are caught as they lie in his bed, and he calls the other gods to witness the sight, having been warned by Helios of Ares' visit. Amid much laughter, Poseidon induces Hephaistos to let his prisoners go, promising to be surety for Ares' payment of the customary damages to the injured husband.

It is well to note that while this story is fairly early, dating from whatever time we suppose the interpolation to have been composed (it has some non-Homeric language), the tales concerning Adonis are all preserved in much later authors and coloured by pretty fancies of Alexandrian and post Alexandrian poetry (cf. p. 154). They may for all that be in substance quite old myths. The cult of Adonis existed in Greece as early as the fifth century B.C. and comprised ceremonial wailings for his death and the preparation of the famous 'gardens of Adonis', shallow vessels containing earth in which seeds were planted to sprout and wither quickly.

The divine twins, APOLLO and ARTEMIS, have an extensive mythology. Their birth was attended with great difficulties owing to the anger of Hera against Leto (cf. p. 36). All the world was afraid to receive Leto when her time grew near, either because Hera had forbidden every place to do so or (this is the version of the 'Homeric' Hymn) because it was known that she would bear a great and terrible god. At last she came to Ortygia, usually but by no means always identified with the island of Delos, which in historical times could point out the very spot where the birth took place; it and Delphoi were Apollo's most famous shrines. Here she was received, either on giving her assurance that her son would greatly honour the place, or as a result of a sort of legal quibble; Hera had said that Leto should not be delivered in any spot on which the sun shone, but Delos was then a floating island and Poseidon kept it covered with water till Leto arrived, thus preventing the sun from shining on it, a pretty tale, but found in no early author; we do not know when it originated. At all events the twins were duly brought to birth; again a probably latish piece of ingenuity makes Artemis the elder (her holy day is the sixth of the month, Apollo's the seventh) and adds that she at once exercised her function of divine midwife and assisted to bring her brother safely into the world.

Naturally, some of the legends are local ones, connected with the cult of Apollo on the island. Thus, as we learn from Kallimachos, whose erudition makes it likely that he is genuinely reporting what the Delians said, a curious rite which consisted in trying, with hands behind one's back, to bite the bark of the sacred olive which Leto had grasped in her birth-pains was explained as being originally a game which the nymph of the island had devised to amuse the baby god. An ancient altar was allegedly composed solely of the horns of wild goats; these were shot by Artemis and the horns put together by Apollo, then four years old. But the twins had more dangerous occupations than these. They set out with their mother to Delphoi, or as it was then called Pytho, where an oracle of the earth-goddess already existed. On the way Leto was assaulted by Tityos, a gigantic son of Earth (according to Homer, but others make him a child of Zeus by one of his numerous loves), and called to her children for help. They promptly shot down her assailant, who thereupon was consigned to Tartaros, where his huge body lies sprawling over nine *plethra* of ground (about 90,000 square feet) and his liver is everlastingly gnawed by two vultures. At Delphoi itself Apollo met a formidable enemy, the dragon Python (in the earliest account, that in the 'Homeric' Hymn to the Pythian Apollo, it was a female), and attacked it with his arrows. Here again someone's ingenuity has been at work. Apollo is one of several gods who were invoked with ritual cries the meaning of which, if they ever had one, had been wholly forgotten. Dionysos for instance was called upon with *euhoi* (a word absurdly written *evoe* and more absurdly pronounced as three

syllables by some moderns). Apollo's cry was *iê* or *hiê* (the *i*
as in Italian, the *e* a broad vowel something like French *ê*).
This sounds not unlike *hiei*, 'shoot!' Hence the tale that the
cry originated in the onlookers crying encouragingly 'shoot,
shoot!' to Apollo as he attacked Python. But this sort of thing
is not really a myth, but merely an instance of the fanciful
etymologies of pre-scientific days; similar guesses are still current among the unskilled. At any rate, Apollo succeeded, and
since the dragon was a sacred creature he had to undergo
purification from the taint of blood. This, his worshippers
believed, was commemorated in the Delphic festival of the
Stepteria. This was held at intervals of eight years, a period
of importance in the regulation of the Greek calendar. Their
months were lunar, and a year of twelve lunar months of
approximately 29½ days each is about 11¼ days short of a
solar year, 354 days instead of 365¼. In eight years the dis-
crepancy amounts to 90 days, and this was put approximately
right by intercalating three lunar months in eight years. Hence
eight years, or even four, came to be thought of as a natural
interval of time, comparable to a year or a month. But to
return to the festival, a band of boys led by one of high birth,
who may have represented Apollo himself, were conducted by
women to a flimsy temporary structure with a table in it, curiously, known as the palace of Python (it is not easy to see
what a dragon was doing with a palace). The table was overset
and the 'palace' burned. The leading boy then was supposed
to go into exile, and he and his followers actually went to the
valley of Tempe, the natural outlet through which the river
Peneios drains the plain of Thessaly. Here they performed
certain rites of purification, and came back crowned with
laurel, Apollo's plant, to which purifying powers were ascribed
in Greek ritual. All this, the meaning of which to its original
inventors is highly uncertain, was thought to be a reminiscence
of the process the god himself had gone through after his
victory over the dragon. It is to be noted that it connotes
no moral condemnation of his action. Any bloodshed *ipso
facto* called for purification, though the killing (for instance
in self-defence) might be entirely justified.

Thus Apollo got possession of the ancient shrine, as it seems
to have been; at all events, its own local legend, happily
preserved for us by Aeschylus, represents it as passing

through the hands of three goddesses, Earth herself, Themis and Phoibe, the last a Titaness, mother of Leto, whose name ('pure bright') obviously resembles Phoibos, the best known of Apollo's own titles. Besides its traditional holiness, it was one of several places which were regarded as the centre of the earth, its *omphalos* (navel); that the earth is approximately spherical and consequently no point on its surafce could be its centre is a scientific discovery very much later than the date of these ancient tales. Zeus himself determined the fact by setting two eagles to fly one from the farthest east and the other from the farthest west, and the point where they met was marked by a stone object, the sacred *omphalos* of which we have many representations in art, although the hope entertained for a while that one of the many wrought stones found by excavators at Delphoi was the *omphalos* has since been shown to be quite unfounded. As already mentioned (p. 28), the typical method of giving oracles was for the god to possess and inspire a woman, the Phythia (woman of Pytho), whose words were then taken down and given (at least in official version) to the inquirer. Apollo also inspired the Sibyl or Sibyls, prophetic women who seem really to have existed and composed oracular works during the archaic period, while later on innumerable pieces of versified forecasts and ritual directions attributed to them were in circulation; those that survive are nearly all as gross and palpable forgeries as any in the world. Generally speaking, any prophet was apt to be connected with Apollo one way or another. For instance, at Olympia, there was a family or clan of diviners who traced their descent from one Iamos, a son of Apollo by a certain Euadne, herself the daughter of a mixed marriage, so to call it, between Poseidon and the Lakedaimonian heroine Pitane. It is likely that some of the tales of this kind are the result of propaganda carried on by the god's active and intelligent Delphic clergy to his greater glory.

But a more noteworthy affiair of Apollo's was his union with Koronis, daughter of Phlegyas, a Thessalian prince. Apollo got her with child, and afterwards detected her in an intrigue with a certain Ischys. In the common story, a raven warned him of this, but Pindar, who tells the tale best, insists that it was his own 'all-knowing mind'. Now the correct conduct, as appears from more than one such legend, for a woman pregnant by a god was to remain chaste till the child was born. Koronis' punishment followed immediately, for Artemis (or, in some versions and less appropriately, Apollo himself) killed her with an arrow. But as she lay on her funeral pyre, Apollo rescued the unborn baby and entrusted it to Cheiron the wise Centaur (see p. 88). Under his tuition ASKLEPIOS, as the child was called, grew marvellously proficient in medicine and remained the patron of that art. According to one myth, which is at least as old as Pindar and Aeschylus, i.e., as the late sixth and early fifth centuries B.C., he was mortal and met his end when the promise of a huge fee tempted him to go beyond the bounds of his practice and revive someone actually dead (there is no agreement as to who it was, but see p. 170). Zeus stopped this interference with the normal course of events with a thunderbolt. But to many of his worshippers, Asklepios was no dead man but a god, and from about the end of the fifth century B.C. his cult was immensely popular. At his shrines, the most famous being that whose imposing ruins are still visible at Epidauros, the sick were either miraculously healed in sleep or given wholesome advice in their dreams, and this was so attractive that the cult yielded but slowly even to Christianity, some of whose saints, notably S.S. Kosmas and Damian, took over the celestial practice. Asklepios was assisted in his beneficent work not only by his sons Podaleirios and Machaon, who are already famous physicians in Homer and make themselves very useful to wounded Achaians when not too busy fighting, but by other members of his family, mostly abstractions with names significant of their functions, such as Hygieia (Health) and Iaso (Cure).

However, the death of Asklepios is part of the older mythology, and led to a strange consequence. Apollo did not dare avenge himself on Zeus, but killed the KYKLOPES who made the thunderbolt. The name Kyklops (Round-eye) covers at least two if not three kinds of monster. In Homer the Kyklopes are a gigantic and savage people, one of whom Odysseus met, to his sorrow (see p. 142). In Heisod and many other authors they are immense one-eyed beings, children of Earth, who are powerful and skilful; they often appear as workers in Hephaistos' forge, and their names are Brontes, Steropes and Arges, i.e., Thunder-man, Lightning-man and

Bright-man. But one Cyclops, to give him the usual form of
the name in modern languages, is the hero of what seems to
be a local Sicilian myth, though he is identified with Odysseus'
captor. He fell in love with a Nereid, Galateia, and his un-
couth love-pleas formed a favourite subject of the lighter
poetry (especially pastoral) from Alexandrian times on. The
victims of Apollo's revenge were of the second type, and he
had to atone for their death by a term of slavery to a mortal.
He became herdsman to Admetos king of Pherai in Thessaly
who perceived that his new thrall was no common herdsman
and treated him with respect. Apollo was grateful, and having
ascertained that Admetos was destined to die soon, he tricked
the Moirai into agreeing that if anyone would take his place
his life might be extended. When no one else would consent
to be his substitute, his wife Alkestis, daughter of Pelias (see
p. 122), volunteered, and accordingly died. But either the
powers of the underworld were so impressed by her virtue
that they sent her back to life, or Herakles (see p. 112) wrestled
with and overcame Death (Thanatos) and made him give up
his prey. It is a moral folktale, the point being that a man's
best friend in need is a good wife. Until Euripides took it as
the subject of the play named after the heroine, it does not
seem to have struck anyone that Admetos' conduct in accept-
ing his wife's sacrifice was thoroughly base. It certainly would
not occur to the original tellers of the tale; a man, a king
at that, is so obviously more valuable than any woman that
the whole thing becomes almost a matter of simple arithmetic,
though the wife's action certainly is laudable to a degree.

Another temporary union of Apollo, this time with a
nymph, resulted in a fully divine son. He saw and was at once
attracted by the valiant huntress Kyrene, daughter of Hypseus
king of the Lapithai, who was battling unarmed with a lion.
Taking her on his chariot he brought her to Africa, where a
famous Greek colony later bore her name, as indeed the
district (the Cirenaica) still does. Her child was ARISTAIOS, an
agricultural deity of some importance, supposed among other
things to have invented bee-keeping.

But he was not always fortunate in his loves. Marpessa,
daughter of Euenos son of Ares, had a suitor Idas, according
to Homer, the mightiest man then alive, who carried her off
and outstripped her father's angry pursuit with the aid of a

team of winged horses given him by Poseidon. Later, while Idas and Marpessa were living in Messene, she was again carried off, this time by Apollo. Idas, himself a great archer, went so far as to draw his bow against the god, and Zeus seems to have recognized his action as just, for he made peace between the two and bade Marpessa choose between them. She preferred Idas, because Apollo, being immortal, might leave her when she grew old.

Kassandra, daughter of Priam king of Troy (see p. 129), was also loved by Apollo, who gave her the gift of prophecy. But after promising him her favours, she finally would not yield to his advances. He could not recall his gift, for a divine gift once given is permanent, but he made it useless to her by dooming her always to be disbelieved although she always prophesied truly. There is a similar story of Apollo and one of the Sibyls, her of Cumae in Italy, which may be modelled on the tale of Kassandra, for it is found in no very early author. She would not yield to him, but he asked her to choose whatever she would and she chose to live for as many years as she held grains of dust in her hand. There were a thousand, and she lived so long, but not having asked to continue young, she shrivelled up till, according to what is clearly a folktale concerning her, she was hung up in a bottle and when asked what she wanted, would answer, 'I want to die.'

An old pre-Hellenic god, worshipped at Amyklai in Lakonia was associated with Apollo in cult, and connected with him in a legend which made him a beautiful boy, although the religious art of the place showed him a bearded man. Apollo made a favourite of the boy, but accidentally killed him with a discus which did not fly straight and struck him on the head. In some, but not the earliest, versions of the story it was blown off its course by Zephyros, the West Wind, who was Apollo's rival. The god somehow contrived that his dead favourite should be deified, and from his blood there sprang up the flower which bore his name, Hyakinthos. It is not our hyacinth, but some kind of flag or iris, red in colour and having marks on its petals which formed the letters AI AI (alas, alas).

Apollo and Artemis acted together in a grim vengeance. Niobe daughter of Tantalos (p. 71) had a number of sons and daughters, and boasted that she was therefore superior to Leto who had borne but one of either sex. Thereupon the

divine twins shot down her entire family, Apollo killing the
boys and Artemis the girls. Niobe wept over them till she
turned into a pillar of stone, which in later times visitors were
shown on Mt Sipylos in Asia Minor. The sudden deaths of
men or boys were commonly ascribed to Apollo, as those of
the other sex were to Artemis.

The twins, or Apollo, removed what might have been a
danger to the gods in the shape of the twin sons of Poseidon
and Iphimedeia, Otos and Ephialtes, otherwise known as the
Aloadai, since Iphimedeia's mortal husband was named
Aloeus. Besides being remarkably handsome, they grew at
so extraordinary a rate that when nine years old they were
nine *orgyiai* or fathoms, i.e., about 54 feet in height, and nine
cubits (about 13½ feet) broad. Though there are sufficient
indications that they were originally some kind of minor deities
or culture-heroes, they commonly appear in myth as enemies
of the gods. They planned to pile Ossa on Olympos and Pelion
on Ossa and so climb up to heaven and make war on its inhabitants. This is the oldest tale, but later ones say that they
wanted Hera and Artemis for their wives. In Homer they are
killed by Apollo, no details being given; a story preserved by
two of the surviving ancient mythographers says that Artemis
changed herself into a hind and ran between them, and in trying to shoot her they shot one another. Their dealings with
Ares are told on p. 51.

Among the adventures of Artemis was one associated with
the earliest star-myth we have from Greece, most of such
tales being of quite late date, when the ideas that the stars are
divine (current in Plato's old age) and of their astrological
influences (astrology comes in after the time of Alexander the
Great, i.e., towards the end of the fourth century B.C. at
earliest) were rife. The constellation Orion was once a mighty
hunter, of whose birth and parentage varying accounts, some
highly fantastic, are given by sundry authors. Placed as he is
in the heavens, he is sometimes represented as pursuing the
Pleiades, or their mother Pleione, but most of his actions are
connected with regions on the earth, especially Boiotia and
the island of Chios. He plainly was of an amorous tempera-
ment, and one of his adventures was his wooing of Merope,
daughter of Oinopion ('Wine-face'; Chios was celebrated for
its wine), whose father he somehow offended bitterly; one or

two later versions of the story give a fully understandable reason, that he had violated the girl. At all events, Oinopion made him drunk and blinded him, but Poseidon (his father in some accounts) had given him the power to walk on the water, and so, with a boy on his shoulders to guide him, he made his way across the sea to the extreme east, where a ray of the sun restored his sight. How he came by his end is variously told. The oldest tale we have, that in Homer, is that Eos (Dawn), always an amorous character, carried him off, but the gods, disapproving, authorized Artemis to shoot him. Other stories are that he tried to violate Artemis herself, or Opis, one of the 'Hyperborean maidens', for whom see p. 49, and she consequently killed him. In the former case it is said that Artemis brought about his death by causing a huge scorpion to grow out of the ground, which stung him fatally, and is now to be seen in the sky as the constellation Scorpius. Other variants abound, some fairly well known, others very obscure, the ultimate reason being perhaps that no important work of literature created a canonical form of Orion's story and so we are left with the remnants of miscellaneous local tales, no doubt eked out with occasional poetical fancies, early or late.

Artemis herself, like all deities, was not to be looked upon casually by mortal eyes, especially when naked. Hence the ill fate of Aktaion, grandson of Kadmos (p. 85). He offended her, and the best-known story of his offence is that he accidentally came upon her as she bathed. She thereupon changed him into the shape of a stag, and his own hounds ran him down and tore him to pieces.

Her attendants were normally nymphs, whom indeed she herself rather resembles, and as already mentioned (p. 27) some of the tales concerning them and their offspring may originally have belonged to the goddess before the idea of her virginity prevailed. The Arkadians traced their origin to a certain Arkas; so far the story is of the most banal kind, for the name means simply 'Arkadian', and to 'explain' the name of a place or people in this fashion is common form in local Greek traditions. But he was said to be the son by Zeus of a nymph, Kallisto, who, in most of the many variations of her story, was changed into a she-bear and either in that form or her own was shot or in danger of being shot by Artemis

herself or by her own son when he grew up and of course
failed to recognize his transformed mother. The bear is, by
the way, one of several wild beasts sacred to Artemis. When
star-myths came into fashion the tale was given a happy ending. Zeus, seeing Arkas about to kill the supposed she-bear,
changed both of them into constellations, and they are still to
be seen in the immortal forms of Ursa Maior and Arctophylax (the Warden of the Bear).

Artemis was identified or associated with sundry goddesses
of nature more or less like her own, for instance BRITOMARTIS
(said to mean 'sweet virgin') of Crete and APHAIA of Aigina,
whose names, meaningless in Greek, give them a good claim
to be considered very old, older than the arrival of the
Achaians. Britomartis was loved by king Minos (see p. 94),
but would have none of him and ran away, till at last she
either leaped from a cliff and was caught unhurt in the nets of
fishers or else simply hid under their nets; in either case, her
title Diktynna was explained from the word for a net, *diktyon*.
She then took passage to Aigina in a fisherman's boat, and
there found refuge from Minos' further pursuit in a grove
sacred to Artemis, after which she received worship under the
name Aphaia. These legends clearly grow out of cult, and the
identification of the two goddesses with one another and
occasionally with Artemis herself indicates that all three
resembled each other more or less closely. At all events,
Aphaia's temple in Aigina is a very solid fact, and the famous
'Aegina marbles' representing scenes from the Trojan War
are its pedimental sculptures. Iphigeneia, for whom see p. 130,
has a name said to be a title of Artemis, and may once more
have begun as a goddess worshipped in two or three districts
of Greece, if indeed she was not originally Artemis herself.

Finally, the twins are both associated with a very singular
and obviously ancient rite. Every year certain cereal offerings
came to Delos, apparently from somewhere north of Greece
and by a circuitous route, being passed on from one community to another until they reached the sacred island. To the
Greeks of historical times they came from the Hyperboreans,
whose name was interpreted as meaning 'beyond the north
wind'. They were said to be a pious and happy people, un-
troubled by war or disease, who worshipped Apollo. It was
further said that certain 'Hyperborean maidens' accompanied

Leto to Delos. There seems to be no consistent tradition of their names and number, but allegedly two of them died on the island and were buried there, contrary to all later custom, for so holy a place must not be sullied by either the end or beginning of life, wherefore neither a birth nor a death, much less a burial, might take place there. In the various lists we have, several names are included which appear as titles of the divine twins themselves, as Opis or Upis, occasionally found as a name or title of Artemis, Loxo, which suggests one of Apollo's most famous titles, Loxias, and Hekaerge, which whether it means Worker from Afar (i.e., archer) or Averter (of evil) is found both in the feminine, as above, and in the masculine, Hekaergos, as titles respectively of Artemis and her brother. Whatever facts underlie the stories of these Hyperboreans, it is clear enough that we have to do with religious customs going back to a very early date.

HERMES was an extremely popular god, and it is no wonder that there were well-known myths concerning him. As he was also the patron of those who won their living by trickery, and was himself the giver of luck, we need not marvel that he is shown in no very dignified or moral light. It is indeed characteristic of Greeks as of many Europeans that they are ready to laugh with and even at their gods on occasion. Hermes then appears especially as inventor and as master-thief. The day he was born he left his cradle, found a tortoise, killed it, and from its shell made the sounding-board of the first lyre. For a while he occupied himself happily playing on it and singing of his own birth and the praises of his mother's household. He then rose and walked from Arkadia to Pieria in Macedonia, arrived there at sunset and stole fifty cattle belonging to Apollo, disguising their tracks and his own. Arrived at the river Alpheios in Elis, he sacrificed some of them to the twelve gods who were later worshipped there, or so it would appear, for the narrative of our best authority, the 'Homeric' hymn to Hermes, is obscure at this point. Having done this and effaced all traces of his sacrificial fire, he went back to his cradle and settled peacefully down till Apollo came looking for his lost cattle. Taxed by him, Hermes argued that he was much too young to know anything about cattle or the theft of them, but was haled away by his elder half-brother to receive the judgement of Zeus, who listened to Apollo's accusation and Hermes' impudent denial of the charge and bade them be reconciled. Hermes was able to soothe Apollo by making him a present of the lyre, and the two became fast friends. Hermes even received from Apollo the gift of a kind of inferior divination, not to be compared with the great oracle of Delphoi.

Apart from this merry tale, Hermes generally, from the Odyssey onwards, appears as messenger of the gods, serviceable to his father, and on occasion to other senior gods, in fact behaving like the well brought up youngest son of a great family. Being a herald, he can go anywhere, including the world of the dead, and one of his functions is that of Guide of Souls (*Psychopompos*), i.e., he escorts the newly departed to the House of Hades. He therefore occurs as a subordinate figure in many stories, but is seldom the centre of any. Now and then he is found mating with a goddess, but as it happens these tales are not found in early authors and so are hard to date, for we do not know to what extent they may be due to the fancy of comparitvely late poets, including the Latins, perhaps working on legends originally told of quite different deities. One which sounds decidedly Oriental, for bisexual beings are not native Greek apparently, is that he had an affair with Aphrodite, who bore a son called after his two parents Hermaphroditos. A naiad called Salmakis fell in love with him, and when he bathed her in the spring she literally united herself to him, wherefore he became bisexual, a hermaphrodite in the physiological sense of the word.

ARES has very little mythology of his own; being a war-god (at least from Homer on; it may be that he was originally a god of death) and also considered a foreigner from Thrace, which he very possibly was, he was generally disliked, for the Greeks, although both a brave and a quarrelsome people, regularly speak with abhorrence of war. He is found in Epic poetry and elsewhere stirring up strife, intervening in battles and so forth, but that is rather part of the poetical machinery than real myth concerning the god himself. He is the lover of Aphrodite, as already mentioned (p. 40), and also of several others; we shall meet with some of his children later. But he is hardly a central figure in any but two or three tales. One is mentioned in Homer; the Aloadai (see p. 47) for some

reason imprisoned him in a chest, where he might have
perished (cf. p. 61) had not their stepmother Eëriboia informed Hermes of his plight, who managed to deliver him.
Another legend, not attested so early but still told by respect-
ably old authors, is presumably a piece of Attic tradition,
one of the accounts of the origin of their ancient court of
justice, the Areiopagos (so called from its place of assembly,
the Areios Pagos or Hill of Ares, near the Akropolis). Ares
had by Aglauros daughter of Kekrops (see p. 86) a daughter
Alkippe, who was violated by a certain Halirrhothios son of
Poseidon. Ares thereupon killed Halirrhothios and was tried
before the court at its first meeting. The jury, whether composed of mortals, or of the Twelve Gods who were worshipped
at Athens, seem to have found him not guilty of murder,
but according to one account, he had, like Apollo (p. 45) to
undergo a period of serfdom for the bloodshed, in other
words he remained subject to the ritual though not the judicial
penalties of his action.

DIONYSOS has a very considerable mythology, and much
of it is concerned with his persecution of impious persons who
would not recognize his godhead and even tried to kill him,
and his terrible revenges on them. It is possible that one cause
at least of this is a vague memory of opposition to his new
and unfamiliar cult. Another is quite probably the nature of
the original cult itself. One of the actions attributed to his
worshippers, apparently with truth, was the rending in pieces
and devouring of an animal. Now Dionysos himself is often
represented as taking bestial shape; at Elis for instance an
ancient hymn addressed him as 'noble bull'. It is neither
impossible nor without analogies from other religions that
it was the god himself who was thus eaten in a kind of wild
sacrament, and that this, being quite unlike any native Greek
way of treating a god, was misunderstood by the framers of
the myths. At all events, dangerous adventures were said to
have been his portion from infancy. His nurses are spoken of
already by Homer. Lykurgos, a Thracian king, pursued them
and him on Mt Nysa, a hill regularly associated with him
(the syllable -*nys*- recurs in his name, whatever it means)
and located by various writers in a dozen different parts of
the world. Dionysos escaped by jumping into the sea, where
Thetis received him kindly, and Zeus blinded Lykurgos, who

died not long after. One named nurse was his mother's sister Ino, who, with her husband Athamas, was driven mad by Hera. In that state Athamas killed one of their children, Learchos, and Ino ran away with the other, Melikertes, in her arms, jumped into the sea, and was transformed into a sea-goddess, Leukothea, her son becoming the minor sea-god Palaimon. But the story is confused and there are many variants; we shall meet with one of them in the Argonautic saga. Ino-Leukothea and Melikertes-Palaimon have their place in cult as well as myth; the former was worshipped in several places, but almost always in ways suggesting that she is connected with the earth and its fruits, not with the sea, and the latter was honoured at the famous Isthmian Games. Clearly neither of these forms of cult has much to do with the story (why should a young girl be called Wrestler, which is what Palaimon means, or be thought specially interested in atheltic sports?), and it must be confessed that we do not know anything like the full facts about mother or son.

Grown to maturity, Dionysos still had many conflicts. When, after bringing his worship to eastern countries, he returned to his birthplace, Kadmos was retired from active government on account of his old age and his grandson Pentheus was king. He flatly refused to see anything divine in the newcomer, and tried in vain to prevent the women from worshipping him. Persuaded by the god (or by a priest of the god), whom he caught and imprisoned, to spy on the women and see what they were doing, he fell into their hands and was torn to pieces, his mother Agaue leading the attack, for in her frenzy she took him for a lion. Another story, told by no one earlier than Ovid, but connected with an old festival, the Agrania, concerns Orchomenos. The daughters of its legendary king Minyas refused to join in the Dionysiac rites, but stayed at home weaving. Dioysos, after disguising himself as a girl and advising them to do as the other women did, performed a series of miracles which drove them mad, and after sacrificing the young son of one of them, they ran out and were turned into bats. Accounts differ as to whether it was Dionysos or Hera who brought madness upon the daughters of Proitos king of Argos, or upon the Argive women generally. In the former story they wandered about the country behaving in unseemly ways and killing their own children;

in the latter, they had offended Hera and imagined that they were cows (Hera's sacred beast; there is a little uncertain evidence that she was very anciently thought of as having the shape of a cow). They were cured by the famous diviner Melampus.

Another attempt on him was made by a crew of Tyrrhenian pirates. They found him alone and attracted by his beauty promptly kidnapped him, hoping to sell him for a slave at a high price. His bonds fell off him, and the pilot, rightly taking this as a manifestation of divine power, warned the rest· who would not heed him. Dionysos then made a vine grow about the mast and the ship to run with wine, while he took the shape of a lion and the unbelievers fled overboard in terror and were turned into dolphins, which ever since have been friendly to man and played around ships.

The conquests of Dionysos belonged chiefly to a late stage of myth, later than Alexander the Great, whose real campaigns furnished a model for the fabulous ones and, in the accounts of them which we have, were themselves sometimes modelled on those of Dionysos. Little time need be spent either on these elaborations or on what is related to them, the fabulous exploits of these two divine and beneficent world-conquerors, especially the Egyptian Osiris, who was often identified with Dionysos.

Dionysos' love affairs are few and unimportant, at least in the genuinely early myths. The only one really worth mentioning is his union with Ariadne, which will be told in connexion with the saga of Theseus (p. 82). This may possibly go back to some very old ritual association of Ariadne, who seems to have been a goddess to begin with, and a god of fertility resembling Dionysos. We know far too little of the religious beliefs and practices prevailing in the eastern Mediterranean before the Greeks came to be dogmatic about such things.

A few stories relate to the god's introduction of his most popular discovery, wine, to various places. Perhaps the best known is that concerning Ikarios, after whom the Attic *deme* (local territorial division) of Ikaria was supposed to be named. In the days of king Pandion (see p. 80) Dionysos arrived and taught Ikarios the use of the vine. He gladly received the instruction and gave some wine to the country people, who drank too much, imagined themselves poisoned, and killed Ikarios. His daughter Erigone, accompanied by her dog Maira, sought and at last found his body and then hanged herself for grief. Some sort of plague or other supernatural visitation impelled the people to seek advice from Apollo, and they were told to honour Ikarios and Erigone, and this was done at a festival the ritual of which included hanging little figures up on trees to swing in the wind. This, whatever its original intention may have been, was a not uncommon rite in various countryside festivals in antiquity, Greek and other; it was interpreted as a commemoration of Erigone's mournful end.

The Satyrs and Seilenoi (see p. 32) were early attached to Dionysos, as is natural seeing that they are minor powers in a sphere where he is great. The Seilenoi especially are often shown as his tutors and attendants; the stone, big enough, says Pausanias in his guide-book, for a small man to sit on, which had served Seilenos for a seat when he came to Athens in the god's train, was shown to tourists on the Akropolis. The Nymphs are also pretty often associated with him, and the ingenious minor poet Meleagros whose epigrams we have in the *Anthology* finds a reason for this; they are powers of water and modify the fierceness of his wine (Greeks were generally very temperate people, and seldom drank their wine neat).

HEPHAISTOS presents one startling difference to the beauty of the other Olympians; he is deformed, having misshapen legs which make him move with a queer, shuffling gait. This is pretty certainly because he had become a god of smiths; now in an early community which had the use of metals the forge would be a natural place of occupation for any man who was otherwise sturdy but lame, whether congenitally or by accident. His slowness, which would make him of little use for hunting, ploughing or warfare, would then matter but little. But part of the god's not very abundant mythology is concerned with the reason for his lameness. One account is that he was lame from birth and Hera was so ashamed of him that she cast him out of heaven; Thetis and Eurynome daughter of Okeanos caught him. Or else Zeus flung him out when he intervened in a quarrel between him and Hera, and he fell on the island of Lemnos, i.e., one of the places which

55

show signs of volcanic activity. Homer knows both stories. However he came by his deformity, his skill seems to have been born with him, and he is credited with making all manner of wonderful things in metal, including impenetrable armour, beautiful jewellery and so forth, and, what is rare among Greek gods, magical objects, such as figures and implements which move of themselves. Here again we may perhaps see an indication of his foreign origin; but the smith is an uncanny person in much purely European folklore, if only because his is a highly skilled trade, needing not only manual dexterity but a considerable knowledge, however rough and ready, of practical metallurgy. His matrimonial troubles and his attempt to marry Athena have already been mentioned (pp. 37, 40). He is not the only divine or at least non-human smith, for not altogether unlike him are two groups of vague beings, the Idaian Daktyloi (Fingers), of either the Cretan or the Phrygian Mt Ida, and the Telchines. Both these groups are credited both with skill in smithcraft and in magic, and the latter at least are regularly thought of as malicious. Both groups also must have had once a large and varied folklore, but we have left only a handful of scrappy, often contradictory statements from which it is not possible to piece together a consistent story. Hephaistos himself does not quite lose his original connexion with volcanic fires, or perhaps it is better to say that he recovers it; one of the explanations why Mt Aetna is volcanic is that his forge is somewhere underneath it and he works there with the Kyklopes (cf. p. 44). One of the products of his workshop is regularly the thunderbolts of Zeus, for until the nature of electricity was known, it was regularly imagined in Greece and elsewhere, that the effects of lightning were the result of some sharp and heavy missile being flung from the sky. Incidentally, that furnished a ready explanation, after the Stone Age was past and forgotten, of any pointed stone tools or weapons which happened to be discovered; they were spent thunderbolts.

As already mentioned, there are not many tales of Pan, and what there are mostly relate to his appearances to mortals on this and that occasion. These include perfectly historical people of known date. One was the famous Athenian runner Philippides ('Pheidippides' is a corruption in some manuscripts of Herodotus, who tells the story, copied by sheep-like mod-

erns; it really occurs only as the designedly absurd name
of a comic character in Aristophanes), while on his way back
from a mission to Sparta, just before the Battle of Marathon
in 490 B.C. He reported that Pan had spoken to him and asked
why he was not honoured by the Athenians, whom he was
ready to help. Another alleged appearance was vouchsafed
to Pindar the great lyric poet. This is not the only vision
which Pindar claimed to have had of supernatural beings, and
we may well suppose that in the one case a man undergoing
the extreme exertion of running from Sparta to Athens, in the
other the exalted imagination of a sensitive artist, caused a
perfectly genuine hallucination. We therefore cannot fairly
classify these tales as myths. A late but famous story, variously
explained, is preserved in Plutarch. The pilot of a becalmed
ship on her way from Italy to Greece was hailed from the
shore by name and on answering, was bidden to announce,
when the ship reached a certain place, that great Pan was dead.
He did so, and was answered by a noise of wailing from the
land. This was reported to the then emperor Tiberius (A.D.
14-37), whose scholars decided that it must be, not the god
Pan himself, who *ex hypothesi* was immortal, but an inferior
supernatural being (*daimon*) of the same name.

The minor powers of the countryside are generally subordinate figures only in myths, and we shall meet them from
time to time in that capacity. Nymphs are frequently thought
of as amorous, regularly as beautiful, and one or two tales of
their unions with men are worth recording, if only because
some few such stories are still told of their modern successors
the Neraidhes (see p. 33). There is a rather vague figure,
Daphnis, a popular subject for later poetry, especially pastoral,
who was a Sicilian herdsman and himself the son of a nymph
by Hermes. Taught music by Pan, he became the father of
pastoral poetry by the pathos and beauty of his laments for
his woes, but as to what those were there is no agreement
among our surviving authorities; the legend was handled by
Stesichoros of Himera in the late seventh or early sixth century
B.C., but we know of his work only through references in late
and not very trustworthy authors. As we have it, there seem
to be two main versions. One was that a nymph became his
mistress, but because he was unfaithful to her with a human
princess, she blinded him. The other, which is the subject of

57

one of Theokritos' best poems, represents him as the enemy of love, punished by Aphrodite with a violent passion which he would not satisfy, so that in the end he died of longing, still taunting and defying the goddess. That he was deified by the agency of his father Hermes seems to be part of the tradition in any case, though not the only conclusion of the story. It is a reminder of how little we really know of local traditions, in this case Sicilian, unless they happen to have attracted the attention of some celebrated writer whose works have come down to us. Another unfortunate affair with a nymph is preserved for us in a scrap of the lost historian Charon of Lampsakos, who wrote in the fifth century B.C. and seems to have been interested in folklore among other things. A certain Rhoikos of Knidos saved an old oak from falling by having it propped up. Its Dryad appeared and thanked him, offering him anything he wished. When he asked for her favours she consented, and told him that a bee would come and inform him when to visit her. It arrived when he was in the middle of a game; he repulsed it rudely, and the Dryad was bitterly offended and blinded him. How old the tale was when Charon recorded it we have no means of knowing.

Several deities have attendants themselves more or less divine who seldom have any myths of their own worth recording. Some, such as Artemis' nymphs, have already been mentioned. Aphrodite is often attended by the Charites (p. 25) and not infrequently by a personification, Peitho (Persuasion), besides her association with Eros. Ares also has two attendant personifications, as old at least as Homer, Deimos and Phobos (Fear and Rout); his title Enyalios tends to become a separate god, or possibly was originally one and was swallowed up in the more vigorous personality of Ares, and there is also a vague war-goddess Enyo. Hades has a large and grim following. The door of his house is kept by a monstrous watch-dog, Kerberos, with several heads (the number is variously given, according to the individual writer's fancy). To approach it, one must cross a water, usually the river Styx, which is a real stream in Arkadia, but alleged to run also in the depths of the earth. The ferry is managed by Charon, represented as a fierce-looking old man. He possibly is an old death-god, and survives in modern belief, usually under the form Charos, but is no longer a ferryman but a rider who carries people off on his horse. It was a not uncommon idea in antiquity that he must be paid for his services, consequently a small coin, at Athens an obol, which was worth about two-pence, was often put in the mouth of a corpse before burial. Some sort of burial, if it was no more than the sprinkling of a little dust over an unburned body, was the essential for admission to the underworld, and various speculations (they can hardly be called myths) as to the fate of the unburied have come down to us. Once across the Styx and in the House of Hades, their lot was a dreary one in the earliest beliefs, as represented in Homer; they led a feeble shallow-life, a faint imitation of their earthly existence, except a few direct of-fenders against the gods such as Tityos (p. 41) who were by nature or had become immortal and so were tormented ever-lastingly in one way or another, like Tantalos, Ixion and Sisyphos (pp. 71, 88, 149). Some few favourites of heaven, on the other hand, never went to the underworld at all, but were carried away without dying to Elysion, or to the Islands of the Blessed, blissful regions somewhere at the ends of the earth, where they were exempt from death and all misfortunes and discomforts and lived in abundance and such happy, self-chosen activities as pleased them. As the Greek moral consciousness developed, the ideas of rewards and punishments based on ethical conduct in this life gained strength; by about the sixth century B.C. Hell, Purgatory and Paradise were fairly familiar concepts. There were judges in the lower world who determined the lot of each new arrival. The ancient Cretan hero-kings Minos and Rhadamanthys (p. 94) are the usual holders of this office; the Athenians added the Aiginetan hero Aikos (p. 91), and there are modi-fications and refinements with which we need not trouble. It was also held, especially by those theorists who believed in reincarnation, that many were given no final and unchange-able state, but either temporarily rewarded or subjected to a process of purification, more or less painful, before commenc-ing a new embodied life. But here we are in the province rather of theological speculation than of myth pure and simple.

In order to have a myth a god need not have a Greek cult. The Sun (Helios) was worshipped nowhere in Greece proper, but only on the island of Rhodes, where no doubt foreign influence had been at work. It was said that Zeus forgot him when assigning lands to the other gods, and Helios was content to wait until Rhodes, which he could perceive rising gradually up under the sea, should come to the surface. He had by the local nymph sons after whom the principal towns of the island were named. Apart from this, he was loved by Klymene, a daughter of Minyas king of Orchomenos in Boiotia. Their son was called Phaethon, and on being told by Klymene who his father was, he set out to visit him. He reached the Sun's abode in the extreme east and on being recognized, asked for a boon, which was granted him unconditionally. It was, to be allowed to drive his father's celestial chariot for one day. Reluctantly Helios consented, but Phaethon was unable to control the divine horses, the sun-chariot quitted its course and the earth was in danger of being burned until Zeus killed him with a thunderbolt and Helios brought the team back on its proper route. Phaethon's sisters wept for him until they became trees dropping amber, and still grow on the banks of the Eridanos (an imaginary river, partly composed of real European ones including the Po), into which his body had fallen.

Selene, the Moon, also had her story, though apart from a false and not very old theory which identified her with Artemis, she was not worshipped by Greeks at all. She loved Endymion, a vague figure said to have founded the city of Elis and to have been extraordinarily handsome. So far, all accounts are in accord, and also that Endymion fell into an endless sleep, but why this happened scarcely any two authors who tell the story agree.

There is another strange little tale, which we can trace back no farther than the second century B.C., but it has an air of being both old and rustic, possibly suggested to some Arkadian peasant by the sight of the moon passing behind a large white cloud. Pan loved Selene, and managed to get possession of her by hiding behind some very fine white fleeces which he apparently invited her into the woods to see. Vergil mentions the story but expresses doubts of its credibility, and his ancient commentators are shocked at its impiety.

Dawn (Eos, Attic Heos and Latin Aurora) is purely mythological and apparently not a goddess of cult in any country. She figures as a very amorous being whose tastes were for handsome young men, not for gods. Among her paramours were Orion (p. 48), Kephalos of Attica and Tithonos of Troy. Kephalos in time left her for his own wife Prokris, concerning whose relations to him we have only a late story flavouring more of novel than of myth or saga. The central features of it, and the only ones which sound as if they were genuine popular tradition, are connected with Kephalos' possession of a javelin which never missed its mark and a hound which always caught its quarry. One day, when hot and tired with hunting, he called to the breeze, *aura* in both Greek and Latin, to come and cool him. Pokris, who jealously fancied he had a mistress somewhere and was spying on him, thought Aura was a woman's name, started, and rustled the bushes in which she was hiding; Kephalos threw his javelin at the sound, supposing it was some beast, and killed her. Again, he joined the huntsmen who were trying to rid Boiotia of a monstrous fox which could not be caught. Zeus settled the impasse by turning fox and hound alike into stone. But Tithonos is Eos' regular consort, and there is a famous story, later than Homer, but found in the hymn to Aphrodite anciently attributed to him and really fairly old. Tithonos asked to be made immortal, but forgot to specify that he should be everlastingly youthful. A divine gift cannot be recalled, so he, like the Sibyl (p. 46), went on living, but became so shrunken that there was nothing left of him but his voice.

In all these myths concerning the gods it is easy to see that they are conceived of neither as spiritual beings nor as exempt from such passions and faults as beset humanity. They never die; that is to say, their souls never leave their bodies, and their bodies are like those of men and women, but larger, stronger and swifter and in all ways superior. They can go immense distances in a few strides, see for hundreds of miles, hear in heaven what is said on earth, and so on; but there is little about them that is magical, except that they can walk invisible to human eyes and take any shape they please, besides disguising human beings in like manner. They are not even essentially immortal, it would appear, but rather made so by their divine food and drink, ambrosia and nektar (idealizations, it may be, of honey and the preparations made from it, such as mead). Ares (p. 52) would have perished in his chest if he had not been rescued. On the other hand, to feed on ambrosia even for a time now and then makes a man immortal. No doubt opinions differer as to exactly how efficacious the divine diet was. Even so, gods can be wounded and then there flows a sort of blood, which Homer calls *ichor*, a word used later in medical language to mean serum. Or they can be knocked senseless by a heavy blow, or otherwise made unconscious. It was not until the great ages of myth-making were past that their occasionally immoral conduct was objected to, as the idea gained ground that there are ethical rules binding on all rational beings alike. It was then that the myths, or some of them, were objected to as teaching bad examples of behaviour, and, according to the taste of the particular reformer rationalized, expurgated, explained as allegories, or flatly denied.

The fact appears to be that the gods, whose worship was a communal affair as a rule, whether the worshippers comprised a whole city-state or some smaller unit within it, were regularly thought of as a sort of superior nobles, an upper class above the human upper classes in whose hands the government of Greek commonwealths of the Mycenaean and archaic periods regularly lay. Therefore early conceptions regarding them were modifications of the ideas entertained concerning human nobles. Many things were possible to a *heros* which would not be tolerated in a commoner. For instance, in all Homer we hear but once of anyone not a noble speaking in an assembly of the whole people. That is Thersites, whose very name became almost proverbial for an insolent fellow with no proper respect for decencies. He rises and abuses Agamemnon in a meeting of the army, presuming it would seem on his position as a kind of licensed jester among the rank and file. Odysseus at once silences him with the help of his staff, and Thersites sits down whimpering. But Achilles abuses Agamemnon to his face, and other nobles contradict and rebuke him on sundry occasions, no one thinking it extraordinary or doing more than suggest that the language used is too violent. Again, it is common enough for nobles to have concubines as well as their lawful wives, and no one objects, nor is the woman blamed by anyone. It is quite the exception when we are told that Laertes, father of Odysseus, had no sexual relations with an attractive maid-servant out of regard for his wife's feelings. But Homer never tells us of such an arrangement in the household of a commoner, nor indeed is it likely that many of them could have afforded it. When we hear of an illegitimate child, the father regularly is known and a noble.

By analogy, the gods have privileges of their own and they are jealous of them and allow no encroachments. To be inspired by a deity is, of course, a highly desirable thing; for instance, it is a great compliment to a minstrel to tell him that it must have been a Muse or Apollo in person who taught him. So with all skills, if the user of them contents himself with modest pride in his abilities and on occasion gives credit where it is due. But it is as imprudent as it is impious to seek to rival the givers of such powers. Thamyris the Thracian minstrel presumed so far as to boast that he could win even if the Muses contended against him in song; whereat they met him, blinded him, and made him quite forget how to sing and play. Diomedes in Homer (p. 134), acting as the agent of Athena and encouraged by her, successively meets and wounds Aphrodite and Ares, but when, without the support of her presence and guidance, he encounters Glaukos the Lykian, he asks him if he is a god, adding that he will not fight the celestial ones, and quoting the story of Lykurgos and his impiety against Dionysos (p. 52). The only hero who can without special divine guidance face gods in fight and not suffer for it is Herakles, and he was even in his mortal life on the way to become a god. Even the great Achilles, himself of divine descent on his mother's side, when Apollo interferes with his slaughter of the Trojans and draws him away from the city by assuming the shape of Antenor and running from him, dares go no further than to reproach the god bitterly and say that he would be avenged on him if he had the power. The Homeric Tartaros contains but few sinners, and one and all have offended directly against the gods or a god. The minor deities were less unapproachable, and on occasion men might take liberties with them. Peleus (p. 89) when he wooed Thetis got her by sheer strength and persistency, wrestling with her and keeping his hold although she assumed all manner of shapes. In this she resembled other powers of the sea, notably Proteus (p. 138). It has to be noted, however, that in both cases the venturesome mortal had been encouraged by a divine revelation, coming in the case of Peleus from the greatest gods, in that of Menelaos from Eidothea, a daughter of Proteus, who might be expected to know her father's temper. Vergil preserves, though with some doubts (after his manner, he inserts a cautious 'if it is worthy of belief' into the narrative), a tale of the vengeance of a sea-creature angered at a slight. Misenus, Aeneas' trumpeter, wandered on the sea-shore near Cumae and invited the Tritons to come and contend with him in making music with their characteristic instrument, the shell-trumpet (*concha*). Thereupon one of them indignantly hurled him into rough, rock-strewn water and drowned him. Vergil's doubts arise, not from tradition, but from the philosophic teachings which had long been current and insisted that deity is superior to such feelings as the Triton's. Centuries earlier, Pindar had more than once expressed incredulity or at all events an unwillingness to discuss or tell stories imputing unworthy conduct to a god; but when the myths were newer and belief in the traditional divinities more naïve, we may fairly assume that the ways of the gods were simply regarded as beyond criticism, much as the doings of a great king are above objections, still more interference, from his underlings, in Homer. Only another god can openly rebuke an Olympian with impunity under any normal circumstances, and even the other gods dare not go too far in dealing with Zeus or his brethren. Not only does Kalypso (p. 144) at once yield up Odysseus at the command of Zeus, although she protests at the unfairness of the greater gods towards amorous goddesses, but even Poseidon, warned by Iris that Zeus forbids him to help the Achaians against the Trojans, blusters for a while and then thinks better of it, in the *Iliad*. Furthermore, gods in popular belief have somewhat the same limitation as fairies in our folktales. What is done by one of them cannot be undone by another; Artemis, in Euripedes, cannot save her favourite Hippolytos, whose death is due ultimately to Aphrodite's anger at his slighting of love; she can only plan to grieve Aphrodite by bringing about the destruction, sooner or later, of some favourite of hers. It is not to be forgotten that Euripedes, a student of the philosophical doctrines then forming, was no implicit believer in the traditional tales but used them as literary material, barely concealing his doubts out of regard for the feelings of his audience.

Hence we can learn from him a good deal about popular, unsophisticated beliefs in his day. Even more, perhaps, can be got from later writers who (cf. pp. 153 ff.) had no belief at all in the ancient ideas concerning diety and were concerned only to tell the stories effectively, without moral or other criticism. So we find, for instance, a completely unfair and ill-tempered Athena in Ovid. He is explaining why the spider (*arachne* in Greek) continually spins and hangs from her web. Arachne was once a woman, very skilled in weaving, who in spite of warnings challenged the goddess to contend with her. Athena consented, and wove a marvellous web portraying the judgements of the gods on the presumptious. Arachne produced a still finer piece of tapestry which showed the illicit loves of the gods. Athena thereupon tore the work and beat Arachne with her batten; Arachne hanged herself for anger and grief, and Athena saved her life and bade her still hang and still weave. The original tellers of such tales doubtless told them with as little attempt at criticism, but with the difference that they believed them, Ovid did not.

A word must be said in passing of a subject very often misunderstood, fate or destiny. There is, in Greek popular thought, no such conception as that of an inexorable, all-governing predestination, impersonal and unaffected by any lesser power. The gods are supreme, within their own limitations. One of these seems to be, that having decided on anything, they feel bound to abide by their own decision; but that they are themselves subject to an impersonal power is not an idea of the age in which the myths were mostly produced, but a philosophical doctrine, especially of Stoicism, many centuries later. Men indeed have their appointment, *moira* or *moros*, according to which they must encounter a certain amount of evil and misfortune, which apparently they cannot avoid but can increase by their own folly. They have their *aisa*, their share (as one might have a share in an inheritance, an assigned amount of the booty taken by an army, or the like), and this again includes a certain amount of ill-luck. But when we find any hint of the origin of these apportionments or shares, it is clear that they come from the gods; indeed a man may almost in the same breath say that it is his *moira* and that it is this or that god who has brought about his defeat and death. In a famous apologue, addressed by Achilles to Priam, we hear of two store-jars which Zeus keeps by him, one full of good things and the other of evil. Most men get some of each, but an occasional unfortunate receives evil only. Against this pre-arranged mixture of good and evil a man may struggle, as Oidipus did (p. 117), but it will be in vain; in some unexpected way the ill-fortune assigned to him will overtake him. Our proverb about the cup and the lip goes back, it would seem, to a much-quoted Greek line, 'many things are between the goblet and the extremity of the lip', and this is illustrated by a story which is rather a cautionary tale than a myth. There was a certain Ankaios, identified by various authors with more than one mythological figure, who planted a vineyard. One of his servants foretold that he would never taste the fruit of it; but the first vintage found him alive and well. He bade the servant bring him a goblet of the newly pressed juice, which the man did, but quoted the verse. Before Ankaios could put the cup to his lips, an alarm came of a huge wild boar ravaging his land; he set the cup down, went out to meet the boar and was killed by it. Evidently it was his individual *moira* to die there and then, and the servant must have had some skill in divination or else prophetic powers. That the future could be known either by inspiration or by the observation of certain signs, e.g., the flight of birds, was believed by nearly everyone in antiquity; but among the many forecasts recorded, those given for example by the oracles, a large proportion are conditional, taking the form 'if such a thing is done, such-and-such consequences will follow'. There is also an occasional mention of the postponement of something decreed. For instance, Kroisos king of Lydia was defeated by Cyrus the Great and his city taken. This was a divine punishment, not for any sin of his own, but for the wickedness of the founder of his dynasty, Gyges, four generations earlier. Apollo, because Kroisos had shown great piety towards him and the gods generally, had done his best to get the disaster postponed till the next generation· but had failed; the Moirai, however, had agreed to put it off for three years, so Kroisos was assured on the unimpeachable authority of Apollo himself. Such, then, were what we may term the mythical ideas concerning fate or destiny.

It is well also to realize in what sort of world the mythical events were supposed to take place. To all peoples in the pre-scientific or pre-philosophical stage of thought, the earth

appears to have the shape which it seems to have in the eyes of
an observer looking at as much of it as can be seen at once.
The Greeks were no exception to this rule. Their earth was a
circular expanse, broken of course by mountains and bodies of
water around which they supposed ran the stream of Ocean
(Okeanos; he and his wife Tethys are the parents of all waters).
Beyond Ocean was the realm of darkness and of the shades of
the dead, at all events in the west; to the extreme east lay the
home of the sun, which he quits every morning to drive
across the sky. Under the earth lay firstly the House of Hades
(Hades is always the god, never his dwelling, until quite late
times), whither the dead went (cf. p. 59). Far below this, as far
from the surface of the earth as that is from the sky, was
Tartaros, a gloomy prison or dungeon in which enemies of
the gods were kept; it developed later into a place of punishment for sinners generally. Above the earth came the solid
vault of the sky, regularly thought of as composed of some
very durable material, such as bronze. Its distance from the
earth, though great, was by no means immeasurable, little if
at all above the summit of Mt Olympus, which is now the
actual abode of the celestial gods, now a sort of vestibule to it.
One reason for this comparative nearness of the heavens was
no doubt that the early Greeks were interested in what we may
call the weather-sky, the upper atmosphere with its clouds.
Zeus is primarily a weather-god, the 'cloud-gatherer', 'hurler
of thunderbolts' and so forth, not a power which makes the
sun, moon and stars go on their courses. Astral religion came
long after the formation of the myths; it was a sort of
by-product of those astronomical researches which led to the
formation of what we call the Ptolemaic theory of the universe,
although it is much older that the great astronomer Claudius
Ptolemaeus. In classical times, the sun, moon and so on were
no doubt gods, but as they remained in their own region and
did not trouble themselves with the doings of mortals, they
were not worshipped, though a pious man might now and
then make a respectful gesture towards the rising sun, for
instance.

What sustained the whole complex of sky, earth and Tartaros was a question which apparently never occurred to the
earlier thinkers. Why the sky did not fall was generally explained by saying that Atlas the Titan held it up (cf. p. 68),

less commonly by naming certain high mountains as its supporting pillars.

As already indicated (p. 14), myths need not concern the gods, but may relate to such things as curious objects in nature. It is hardly too much to say that there was not one outstanding physical feature of their environment, not an odd-shaped rock, a striking hill or cliff, to which the ancients did not sooner or later attach some story. Flowers again had their myths. Thus, the narcissus was once a very handsome young man, by name Narkissos, who for some reason fell desperately in love with his own reflection in a pool of water and pined away and died for unsatisfied longing. He was turned into the flower which still bears his (pre-Greek) name. The story may be connected with the widespread belief that a mirror-image of any kind is or at least can affect the soul of the person mirrored. The famous vale of Tempe (p. 42) was cut by Poseidon. A small rocky island was apt to be explained as a missile hurled by some god at a giant or other enemy. The story of Niobe turning into a rock has already been told (p. 47); it is but one of several like tales, starting from a fancied resemblance of a rock-formation to a human or animal shape. We shall meet with an example in the legend of Perseus (p. 103). Trees, as we have seen (p. 39), might originally have been human beings. The Titan Atlas, who after the victory of the gods was set to hold up the sky, was identified with the mountain range in Africa which still bears his name ('the much-enduring'). When we consider that Ovid, following Greek models, wrote fifteen books of stories of this kind, the famous *Metamorphoses,* it is clear that no complete list of them can be given except in a much longer and more detailed work than this. Rivers were regularly sacred, commonly personified as, or supposed to be the dwelling-places of, gods either bull-shaped or bull-headed, and a number of insignificant stories professed to explain how this or that stream got its name; someone whose work has descended to us along with Plutarch's writings composed a little treatise on this subject. A few myths are of more importance. We shall meet some of them in connexion with other tales, for instance the adventures of Herakles (see p. 115). The following at all events is famous enough to be told for its own sake. Alpheios, the river of Elis, fell in love and pursued the object of his desires, who in some forms of the story was Artemis herself, but in the best-known version the fountain Arethusa. She plunged into the sea to escape him, and he followed, till at last the pursuit ended at Syracuse, where there was a spring of that name and it was believed that the waters of the Alpheios ran into it underneath the sea, preserving their freshness all the way.

III

SAGAS

IT has already been mentioned (p. 13) that all the great cycles of saga originate in Mycenaean times and are associated with Mycenaean sites. This gives us a handy classification of them, and we begin with the Argolid, the region which contains the ancient cities of Argos, Mycenae and Tiryns. The stories group around dynasties, probably real however much clouded in fables, of old days, and the chief of these was the Pelopidai. According to all tradition they were foreigners, descendants of Tantalos king of Sipylon in Asia Minor. This prince was proverbial for his wealth until Kroisos, the historical king of Lydia, supplanted him; he also was admitted to the society of the gods, entertained at their tables and was himself on occasion their host. But in Pindar's words 'he could not digest this great good fortune', and offended them beyond pardon. What his crime was is variously told; one of the most notorious tales is that to test their omniscience he murdered his own son Pelops and cooked his flesh for the feast. The horrible nature of the food was quickly discovered, and the child restored to life. Part of one shoulder, however, had been eaten by Demeter, then distraught with grief at the loss of Kore (p. 34), and this was replaced by a shoulder of ivory. Another version is that he stole nektar and ambrosia and gave them to his human companions. In any case, everlasting punishment fell upon him, the fruit of his ill-fated immortality. In some accounts he is forever hungry and thirsty; he stands in a pool of water up to his chin, but whenever he tries to drink, it drops away from him. Overhead are boughs laden with ripe fruit, but when he reaches for it the wind blows it away. This is the origin of our word 'tantalize', which is not ancient, though a simile from Tantalos' punishment is found in Plato. Another account is that he is doomed to everlasting fear. He reclines at table, but

71

over his head is a huge rock which always seems just about to fall and crush him.

However, his son Pelops grew and prospered. He left his native country for that part of Greece which was named after him the Peloponnesos ('Pelops' island'; it is actually a peninsula). Here he found that Oinomaos king of Elis had a fair daughter Hippodameia whom he did not wish to see married. Anyone who liked had his leave to woo her and carry her off in his chariot, but Oinomaos always pursued with his spear and had already killed a dozen suitors or so when Pelops came forward. He took a double advantage of Oinomaos, for he used a winged team provided him by his lover Poseidon and also bribed Oinomaos' charioteer Myrsilos or Myrtilos (the name sounds curiously like the royal Hittite name Mursil) to take out the linch-pins of his master's chariot and replace them with wax, with the result that Oinomaos was thrown and killed when the vehicle collapsed under him. Pelops then cheated Myrsilos of his reward and flung him into the sea, thus bringing a curse on his line which persisted from generation to generation. Hippodameia bore him several sons, the best known being Atreus and Thyestes. The former became king, but Thyestes seduced his wife Aërope and stole the golden ram which was the pledge of kingship, a gift from the gods to the royal house. Atreus, however, was victorious in the struggle which followed and banished his brother. Afterwards he recalled him, pretending a reconciliation, invited him to a feast and there served up to him the flesh of two of his three young sons, afterwards showing him their heads, hands and feet (the feet of the Pelopidai are consistently represented as of peculiar shape, and it is to be remembered that to any nations who, like the Greeks, wear no stockings and are shod mostly with sandals, the feet are much more conspicuous than with us). Thyestes cursed his brother and all his line, and departed with his infant son Aigisthos. There is a still more horrible version of the tale in which, being warned that the only possible avenger would be his son by his own daughter Pelopia, he violated her, she bore Aigisthos and exposed him, but he was suckled by a she-goat (*aix*), rescued and named from that circumstance.

Whether the result of incest or not, Aigisthos grew to manhood and carried on the family feud. While Agamemnon, son of Atreus and his successor, was absent at the Trojan War

(p. 130), Aigisthos seduced his wife Klytaimestra, sister of
Helen, who in the post-Homeric tradition had a reason of her
own for hating her husband, the sacrifice of Iphigeneia (p. 130).
When Agamemnon returned, he was received with all out-
ward welcome and respect, and then set upon and murdered.
In Homer, this was on Aigisthos' land, to which he had been
driven by bad weather; later, it was in his own palace at
Mycenae, or Argos, which, being much the more important
place in classical times, is constantly confused with it. With
him perished Kassandra (p. 46), who had been assigned to
him as his gift of honour (*geras*) out of the spoils of Troy.

The duty of avenging the murder now devolved upon the
only son of the marriage of Agamemnon and Klytaimestra,
Orestes, who was still young when his father was killed. The
saga here correctly reflects the condition of the time before
regular courts for the trial of homicide existed and the blood-
feud was a family affair. Also, in such an age the duty of
dealing with the misdoings of any woman within the family
fell upon the senior male of the house. It therefore was the
manifest business of Orestes to punish both Aigisthos and his
mother, and in the earlier tradition there are no two opinions
about his conduct in putting both of them to death; it was a
worthy deed and he gained much credit thereby. But later
ages introduced another element, the implacable pursuit of
Orestes by the Erinyes (p. 19), whose part it was to punish
the shedding of kindred blood, or other grievous harm done
to anyone nearly related, regardless of the doer's motive.
Hence there is a variety of accounts of how Orestes finally got
rid of his tormentors. The best known, because it forms the
subject of Aeschylus' *Eumenides*, is that Orestes stood trial before the Areiopagos, then meeting for the first time under the
presidency of Athena herself (contrast p. 52), and was acquit-
ted by her casting-vote. The Erinyes were reconciled by
Athena's persuasive eloquence, and became the Eumenides, or
Well-disposed ones, actually a quite different group of deities
whose province was rather the fertility of the earth than the
punishment of wrong-doers. But there are several other versions known and there may well have been others still of which
no record has come down to us. Orestes himself becomes a
rather indistinct figure after this great event. He generally is
said to have married his cousin, Hermione daughter of Mene-

73

laos and Helen, and the dynasty apparently was thought to have lasted till the coming of the Dorians to the Peleponnesos, that is till about the twelfth or even eleventh century B.C.

Menelaos was the brother of Agamemnon and generally represented as king of Sparta, that is the old Mycenaean town north of the river Eurotas; the historical Dorian Sparta lies south of it. Like his brother's name, his is good Greek; Agamemnon is 'very steadfast' (sc., in battle) and Menelaos (in Attic *Meneleos*), 'he who stands up to a *laos*', that is to the whole following of a chieftain. Both names are very understandable for members of a warlike aristocracy. The central point of his career was his marriage with Helen (*Heléne*, in Doric *Heléna*). Concerning her origins, we need hardly doubt that she is pre-Greek, for her name means nothing in their language and the suffix -*na*- which she shares with Athena (p. 27) points in the same direction. There is also some evidence that she began as a tree-goddess. However, in our tradition she was a human princess, though of partly divine parentage. Zeus loved Leda, wife of Tyndareos king of Sparta, and approached her in the form of a swan. She laid an egg, and from it were hatched one or more children; or she laid two eggs, or the eggs were not laid by her at all, but by Nemesis, a minor goddess worshipped at Rhamnus in Attica, who fled from Zeus' advances but was at last caught by him in bird-form after a transformation-race. In this case the eggs, or an egg, were or was hatched by Leda; or again, some of her children were normally born. Apart from this grotesque feature, unusual in a Greek story, the tradition is tolerably constant; Leda had two daughters, Helen and Klytaimestra, and twin sons, Kastor and Polydeukes (the Latins corrupted his name into Pollux). Of these, Helen and Polydeukes are consistently said to be the children of Zeus, Klytaimestra and Kastor of Tyndareos. Here we have the influence of a very widespread and ancient belief found among many peoples, namely that twins always have different fathers, one of them supernatural, a god or spirit of some kind. After Homer, to whom Kastor and Polydeukes are mortal, the Dioskuroi (sons of Zeus) as they are called regularly, are the objects of cult in Sparta and elsewhere and share immortality between them. They were notable athletes and warriors, Kastor being a great horseman and his brother a magnificent boxer. Grown to manhood, they carried off the daughters of a certain Leukippos (the name is one of several stopgaps in Greek myth and genealogy, for it means simply a wealthy and important person who can afford to keep showy white horses for no practical purpose), Hilaeira and Phoibe, who were betrothed to their cousins, Idas and Lynkeus. These pursued the Dioskuroi, and in the fighting Kastor was killed. Polydeukes besought Zeus to let him share his immortality with his brother, and his prayer was granted. Kastor came to life, and the twins are now always together, spending alternate days in heaven and under the earth. Or they are never together, one of them being always in the one place and the other in the other, day about. With Helen they form a group of a kind common in and around Greece, a goddess with two male attendants, and they are responsible for the electrical phenomenon known as St Elmo's fire. If two such fires appeared on board a ship in a storm, it was a good sign; the Dioskuroi were come to her rescue. But one fire, which meant that only Helen was there, was an evil omen.

Helen from her childhood was of extraordinary beauty, and when she grew to marriageable age, her suitors were many. Tyndareos, on the advice, in some accounts, of Odysseus, made all the wooers swear that Helen should have free choice among them and those who were rejected would if need were champion the cause of her and her husband. She chose Menelaos, and when Paris carried her off (p. 129), the rest kept their oath and followed Agamemnon to the war against Troy. Klytaimestra meanwhile had married Agamemnon.

Occasionally the Dioskuroi were active in aid of their worshippers on land as well as at sea, and Helen had to her credit a pretty miracle, which may serve to offset her bad repute in other respects. In Italy, the city of Lokris was at war with its more powerful neighbour Kroton, and vainly sought military aid from Sparta, which, however, sent them the Dioskuroi, presumably in the form of emblems of some kind (it was common to represent them with a primitive object shaped something like a football goal, known as *dokana*). Joining battle at the river Sagra against an army much larger than their own, the Lokrians saw two men on white horses, wearing the red cloaks of Spartan soldiers, on their flanks, and won a decisive victory; whence a proverb equivalent to 'strange but true' came into circulation; it was, 'truer than what happened at the Sagra'. Helen's miracle was the following. A noble Spartan family had a baby daughter of revolting ugliness. Her nurse used to take her daily to the shrine of Helen and pray before the cult-image that her looks might be improved. One day a lady appeared, insisted on seeing the child, stroked her head and promised that she should become the most beautiful woman in Sparta. This came true, and the girl lived to be the wife of one Spartan king and mother of another.

Generally speaking, however, Dorian Sparta had very little to add to the older Achaian myths and sagas. The Dorians seem to have been an unimaginative people, at least at their arrival in Greece late in the second millennium B.C., and for the most part to have appropriated the older tales by one transparent device or another, notably the legend of Herakles, which will be dealt with in the next chapter.

Arkadia, the hilly interior of the Peloponnesos, which provided a refuge for the native population from the Dorians and was never entirely subject to them, kept something of its own culture and its peculiar and archaic dialect. It was rich in very strange cults of a sort which the more advanced regions of Greece had outgrown or modified, and had various strange tales to tell. One of them related to the flood already mentioned (p. 24). The immediate cause of the anger of Zeus was the impiety of Lykaon, a somewhat dim figure whose name seems to connect him with Mt Lykaion and the ancient cult of Zeus there. Zeus was his guest, and, like Tantalos in one version of his story (p. 71), he tested the god's omniscience by serving human flesh, for which he was slain with a thunderbolt and the flood began. The cult itself had unusual features. Rightly or wrongly, the ancients supposed that the name of the mountain and the god's own title of Lykaios had something to do with the word for a wolf, *lykos,* and the result was a story of werewolves which seems to have had several forms in the mouths or under the pens of various tellers. It is at least as old as the fourth century B.C. and may be much older. Putting the various accounts together, we learn that the sacrifices to Zeus Lykaios included a human victim, and whoever tasted of his flesh turned into a wolf. Or there was no human sacrifice involved, but a member of a certain family was chosen by lot and led to a pool of water, where he stripped, hung his clothes on an oak, swam across and emerged in wolf-form. In either case he must remain a wolf for nine years, but in the tenth, if he had not tasted human flesh in all that time, he regained his own shape. Another Arkadian shrine had its cautionary tale. Poseidon, who was widely honoured in Arkadia and not infrequently in horse-shape and as the consort of an earth-goddess identified with Demeter, had a temple at Mantineia entrance to which was forbidden. It had, however, no material barrier except a cord stretched across the entrance. One man, a certain Aipytos, ventured to break the cord and go in, and for his impiety was promptly stricken blind and died not long afterwards. At Tegea, an elaborate story was attached to a priestess of Athena, by name Auge: like Helen, she may have been originally a goddess. But as we have her legend, she was the daughter of the local king, Aleos, who was warned by the Delphic oracle that if she bore a son he would himself be killed by him. He therefore made her priestess and threatened her with death if she were unchaste. Violated by Herakles, she bore a son Telephos, and her father, on discovering what had happened, exposed the baby on Mt Parthenion and put Auge into a chest which he cast into the sea. But Athena caused the chest to land safely at the mouth of the river Kaïkos in Asia Minor, where Auge was rescued and became the wife of a local prince. Her child either was in the chest with her or was later re-united to her after some subsidiary adventures. He had in either case been suckled by a deer. Becoming a king of Mysia, he had the encounter with Achilles which will be told in connexion with the Troy-saga (p. 130).

Elis had several local legends, apart from the conflicting stories of how the famous Olympic Games were founded, (cf. p. 112). Besides being the adopted country of Endymion (p. 60), it numbered Salmoneus among its former rulers. He was a son of Aiolos (p. 89), and it would seem that originally he had a reputation as a great rain-maker, who could bring on a real storm by imitating the noises of one. But in tradition his weather-magic came to be misunderstood and he appears as a blasphemously presumptuous man, who drove about in his bronze chariot mimicking the noise of thunder by its rattling and flinging torches to imitate lightning, i.e., pretended to be Zeus and claimed worship accordingly: whereat the real Zeus smote him with his thunderbolts and he is now in Tar-

taros. Pausanias, in his invaluable guide-book to Greece
(second century A.D.), has preserved a most remarkable legend
of a divine intervention, the *hieros lógos* of a strange local
cult. The Arkadians, he says, had invaded Elis and the Eleans
went out to do battle with them. When they were drawn up,
a woman with a baby at her breast approached their leaders
and told them that she was the child's mother and had been
warned in a dream to give him to them as their ally. They
accordingly laid the child naked in the forefront of their army.
The Arkadians advanced; the child became a serpent, and the
Arkadians fled in terror, the Eleans pursuing them and gaining
a complete victory. The serpent child was thereafter worshipped by the name Sosipolis, i.e., saviour of the city.

Corinth does not seem to have been rich in local legends,
but was active in appropriating those of other regions. Thus
it claimed a large share in the saga of the Argonauts (p. 121),
which its epic poet Eumelos dealt with. It also claimed
Bellerophon, who Homer says was a native of a place called
Ephyre in the Argolid. The Corinthians identified this with
their city, and thus Bellerophon became a Corinthian in post-
Homeric tradition. He was famous for two adventures, the
first of which is pure *märchen*, recurring elsewhere in Greek
tradition (pp. 83, 89) and in the Hebrew saga of Joseph. The
king of the Argolid was called Proitos. His wife, Anteia in
Homer, Stheneboia in later tradition, had a passion for Bellerophon, and being repulsed by him, for he was chaste, accused
him to her husband of trying to violate her. Proitos had
scruples about killing him, but sent him away to his father-in-
law the king of Lykia, called Iobates after Homer, but not
named by him, with a letter asking for the bearer to be put to
death. Iobates again would not murder him, but sent him on a
series of perilous adventures, hoping that he would find his
death in one of them. He first bade him kill the Chimaira
(literally she-goat or kid), a thoroughly non-Greek, Oriental
monster, having the head of a lion, the hinder parts of a
dragon and a goat's body between. Bellerophon succeeded, and
was then sent against a hostile tribe, the Solymoi, whom he
overcame. Thirdly, he was bidden to fight the Amazons. These
were a warrior race consisting of women; they recruited their
numbers by temporary unions with men of neighbouring
peoples, keeping their female children and sending the boys

away to their fathers. Their habitat is regularly somewhere on the boundaries of the world as known to the Greeks, and therefore shifts as geographical knowledge improves; sundry places in Asia were said to be former homes of the Amazons. They were horsewomen, armed with bows and light battle-axes. These too Bellerophon overcame, and also killed a party of picked Lykians who were sent out to ambush him. Iobates now recognized that his guest was no ordinary man and married him to his daughter, whereby Bellerophon became the ancestor of a line of Lykian princes. But misfortune overcame him; Homer does not say why, but later writers take up the story. While still in Corinth, Bellerophon succeeded after long endeavours and with the help of Athena, who sent him in a dream a wonderful bridle, in taming the winged horse Pegasos (p. 34), and it was on its back that he won his victories, and also had revenge on Stheneboia, whom he took up with him and then flung off. But he grew too proud, and tried to fly up to heaven. Pegasos thereupon threw him off, departed to his own place among the gods, and Bellerophon, lamed by the fall, spent the rest of his days in misery. Bellerophon, who probably is originally no Greek but an Asian and indicates early connexions between Corinth and the East, had a famous ancestor Sisyphos, of whom we shall hear more in dealing with *märchen*.

Megara has its legend also. When Minos (p. 82) was making war on Athens he also attacked Megara, which however was magically impregnable, for its king Nisos had a purple lock of hair and as long as that remained uncut, no enemy could take his city. But his daughter Skylla (not the same as Odysseus' sea-monster, see p. 143) fell in love with Minos, and to win his favour cut the fatal lock while Nisos was asleep. Minos took the city, but in abhorrence of her unnatural treachery he dragged her behind his ship when he set off for Crete. Hereupon the gods intervened; Skylla was turned into a bird called *keiris* or *kirris,* as yet unidentified, and Nisos into a sea-eagle which pursues it. It is noteworthy that practically the same story is told of Amphitryon the nominal father of Herakles (p. 105). When he was fighting the Teleboans, their king Pterelaos could not be killed so long as a single golden hair which grew in his head remained in place. His daughter Komaitho fell desperately in love with

79

Amphitryon and pulled out the hair; Pterelaos was killed and Amphitryon put Komaitho to death. Once more, we have a *märchen* intruding into a saga.

Athens has a number of stories, mostly connected with her legendary kings. These form a very confused group who cannot be joined into one genealogy or dynasty; it is of course possible that the monarchy, while it lasted, passed through the hands of several different families. Erichthonios has already been mentioned (p. 37); another very early name is that of Kekrops, whose daughters, Aglauros, Herse and Pandrosos (Bright, Dew, All-dewy) no doubt were originally minor goddesses concerned with providing the necessary moisture for the thin Attic soil. They had a cult, but their story such as it is has already been told. Their father was born from the earth and appropriately enough was partly serpentine in shape; the snake is the typical chthonian creature. Erechtheus, with whom Erichthonios is often confused, is connected in legend with Poseidon and may indeed have originally been a local form of him. He again is know largely in connexion with his daughters. Attacked by Eumolpos of Thrace, who allied himself to the then hostile people of Eleusis (there was a priestly clan of Eumolpidai at Eleusis in historical times), he discovered that the only way to defeat him was to sacrifice a daughter. His wife Praxithea consented, his daughter Chthonia was a willing victim, Eumolpos was defeated and killed by Erechtheus, but Poseidon, who was Eumolpos' father, brought about the death of the king and all his surviving family.

Another king, Pandion, had two daughters, Prokne and Philomela. The former married Tereus, son of Ares and king of Daulis in Thrace, who also fell violently in love with Philomela and after seducing or raping her, cut out her tongue to prevent her giving information, and imprisoned her. She contrived to get a piece of needlework on which she had recorded her misfortune sent to her sister; the two then conspired against Tereus and served him the flesh of his son Itys or Itylos at a meal. Discovering what had been done, he tried to kill the sisters, but all three were turned into birds, he into a hoopoe, Prokne into a nightingale and Philomela into a swallow; which explains why the hoopoe's crest suggests a diadem, the nightingale sings sadly (she is lamenting her child; it was not till comparatively recently that it became known that the female nightingale cannot sing at all), and the swallow chatters (having no tongue, she cannot speak plainly).

Either Erechtheus or Pandion had a daughter Oreithyia, who was carried off by Boreas, the North Wind, and bore him two sons, Zetes and Kalaïs, who had wings on their feet and so could fly like their father. There were also other children of the marriage, but none of importance.

Pandion again (the mythological chronology becomes confused here and some ingenious ancient corrected it by supposing that there were two kings of that name) had several sons, one of whom, Aigeus, became after sundry adventures king of Attica, but had no children. Misinterpreting an oracle which told him how to remedy this lack, he had an intrigue with Aithra daughter of Pittheus, king of Troizen. Another tale is that her lover was Poseidon, which is probably the same story over again, for Aigeus, after whom the Aegean Sea was supposed to have been named, is in all likelihood no king but a local sea-god originally. At all events she bore a son Theseus, who on reaching manhood performed a feat of strength devised by Aigeus, to turn over a heavy rock and so recover a sword and a pair of sandals buried under it. He then set out for Athens, insisting on going by land, as that was by far the more dangerous route, being infested by brigands and other enemies of mankind. He encountered and overcame in turn Periphetes, otherwise Korynetes (Club-wielder), near Epidauros, whose club he took; Sinis, otherwise called Pityokamptes (Pine-bender), who used to tie his victims to two pines, which he bent down, and then tear them in two by letting the trees fly up again; the Grey Sow of Krommyon on the borders of Megara; Skeiron, who used to make passers-by wash his feet and flung them over a cliff as they were doing so; Kerkyon of Arkadia, a wrestler, who lived at Eleusis; and finally, near Athens, Damastes, otherwise Prokrustes (the Stretcher), who laid his prisoners on his bed and if they did not exactly fit it, racked them out or lopped them till they did. Several of these rascals he served as they had served others. Arriving at Athens, he was in danger of been poisoned by Medeia (p. 128), who had taken refuge there after her flight from Corinth, but Aigeus recognized him in time and dashed the poisoned cup from his hand, whereupon Medeia fled. Theseus then successfully defended his father against his cousins, the sons of Pallas (the name, which is masculine, has a different accentuation and declension from the title of Athena, p. 37; this Pallas was a brother of Aigeus), who were plotting against him. Next came his greatest adventures. Herakles had let the Cretan Bull (p. 108) loose near Marathon, and Theseus caught it and sacrificed it to Apollo. On the way thither he was hospitably received by a poor old woman named Hekale, and on his return found her lying dead. By his directions she was thenceforth worshipped; it is the *aition*, as a Greek would call it, that is to say the traditional explanation, of a local cult.

But the greatest adventure of all came shortly after. Minos, whose son Androgeos had been murdered in Attica, had made war on the Athenians and reduced them to make peace under hard conditions; every year they must send him seven youths and seven maidens, whom he shut up in the Labyrinth (p. 95), to starve there or be killed by the Minotaur. Theseus volunteered to go as one of the youths. On arrival, his beauty attracted the attention of Minos' daughter Ariadne, who managed to give him a sword and a clue of thread, by means of which he could find his way out of the maze. He met and killed the Minotaur, escaped with the other intended victims, and fled by sea with Ariadne, Minos for some reason not pursuing them. Probably if we had the full tale, which at this point is certainly *märchen*, not saga, we should find that it was a magic flight of the pattern familiar from many folktales, and that Minos was stopped by magical articles of some kind thrown in his way. The usual story goes on in like strain. Theseus and Ariadne landed on the island of Dia (Naxos), and there he completely forgot her and sailed on without her. She, however, was found and wedded by Dionysos. Still forgetful, Theseus approached Athens with black sails on his ship, and did not replace them with white ones, as he had arranged to do if he succeeded. Aigeus, seeing the sails and supposing that his son was dead, leaped into the sea and was drowned. Again, if we had the full story we should no doubt find that Theseus had violated some magical tabu and his loss of memory was the consequence of it. Greeks as a rule thought little of magic, and it is a comparatively rare feature in their stories, at any rate in those which became well-known themes of literature.

Theseus

Once more we find Theseus' parentage dubious. There is an episode of his voyage to Crete which depends on his being son of Poseidon. Minos was on board the ship and, making too free with one of the girl-prisoners, was checked by Theseus. He boasted of his descent from Zeus, who thundered to confirm his son's words. Theseus claimed Poseidon for his father, and Minos thereupon threw a ring overboard and challenged him to recover it. He promptly sprang overboard, was hospitably received by Amphitrite (p. 34) and returned to the ship with the ring.

The rest of Theseus' story is concerned mostly with his exploits as king, the chief one being the *synoikismos* ('united settling'), i.e., the establishment of Athens as the sole centre of government, the lesser settlements of Attica coninuing as villages with a communal life of their own but no say in the general affairs of the nation, domestic or foreign. This is a real event, and must have been brought about by someone, whether a king named Theseus or not; it is therefore a fragment of genuine history embedded in the legend. Other activities of Theseus are mere fable, mostly modelled on the better-known and older saga of Herakles (p. 104), whose friend and comrade he is said to have been. Together they made war on the Amazons (cf. p. 108), and for that reason or some other these invaded Attica, encamping in the very heart of it at the Areios Pagos (cf. p. 52). The Athenians defeated them after a hard struggle, and their leader, Hippolyte or Antiope, was captured and married by Theseus, to whom she bore a son Hippolytos. After her death he married Phaidra, sister of Ariadne, who fell violently in love with Hippolytos, and being repulsed by him, falsely accused him in a letter to her husband and then hanged herself. Theseus (again we touch *märchen*) had been granted three wishes by his father Poseidon, and used one of them in the form of a curse on Hippolytos, whom he banished. As the young man drove away from Troizen, where he was living at the time, a sea-monster frightened his horses, who upset the chariot and dragged him. Dying, he was reconciled to his father, who had by this time found out the truth; in Euripides' famous play it is revealed to him by Artemis, who loved Hippolytos for his zeal in hunting and his chastity. Most of the other tales concerning Theseus are *aitia,* explanations of old rites and customs as commemorating this or that event in his career; but the story of his end is so unlike the usual triumphant close of a hero's career as to suggest another scrap of genuine history. He was dethroned by a rebellion against him, headed by one Mnestheus, who in Homer is the leader of the Athenian forces before Troy. Going to the island of Skyros, he either was murdered or died by accident there, and some bones alleged to be his were brought back to Athens by the fifth-century statesman Kimon, one of many cases of a State going to considerable trouble to get relics of an ancient worthy, native or foreign, in order to enjoy the benefits of a *heros* or powerful ghost buried and honoured on its territory.

Athens claimed to be the *metropolis* or mother-city of all Ionians, that is of those inhabitants of Greece proper who left their country and went to Asia Minor when the Dorians invaded. The claim was justified by another legend. Erechtheus had a daughter Kreusa (another stopgap name, meaning simply 'princess' or 'queen'), who had a son by Apollo. She married Xuthos, a son of Hellen, the eponymous ancestor of all Hellenes (Greeks), but they were long childless, and Xuthos, consulting the oracle at Delphoi, was bidden to take as his son the first person he met on leaving the temple. This was Kreusa's child, exposed by his mother and rescued by Apollo, and because he found him while going (*ión*) from the shrine, Xuthos named him I'on, and he became the ancestor of the Ionians. It is a rather feeble piece of amateur etymology, and the story is known chiefly because Euripides used it as the subject of a well-known play. Apollo's share in it is due to his having been one of the most prominent gods in Ionian worship, their great festival, the Panionia, taking place at Delos.

Historical Athens had no real kings, though one of the annual magistrates (*archontes*) bore the title of king (*basileus*) and performed certain sacral functions which doubtless had belonged to the kings in their time. Kingship seems to have passed quietly away, for the story of how it came to an end is creditable to the last occupant of the throne, Kodros. The Peloponnesians invaded Attica in his time, and it was foretold that whichever party lost its leader first would win. He therefore disguised himself as a rustic, went into the hostile camp, picked a quarrel with a soldier and was killed by him. The victorious Athenians were so impressed by his patriotism that they decided to have no more kings, as they could not hope for another as good.

Boiotia was rich in legends, the most important of which cluster around the saga of Thebes, to be told in the next chapter. Apart from this, we have the tale of the foundation of the Theban citadel, the Kadmeia. Kadmos was a brother of Europê (p. 94), and after long and vain search for his sister he arrived in Boiotia, where he was bidden by the Delphic oracle to take a certain cow for his guide, building his city where she lay down. This she did at the site of the future Thebes, and he then sacrificed her to Athena, and therefore needed water, thus coming into conflict with a formidable dragon which guarded the only available spring. He fought and killed it, and by Athena's advice sowed its teeth, which at once grew up as armed warriors. Again by advice of the goddess, he pelted them with stones, and they, each supposing that he was attacked by some of his comrades, fought one another until only five were left, who became the ancestors of the Theban nobility, the Spartoi (interpreted as 'sown men'). After going into servitude for a time to atone for the blood-guilt of the dragon's death (for it was a sacred creature, child of Ares himself in some accounts), he returned, married Harmonia, daughter of Ares and Aphrodite, and had by her four daughters, Ino, Semele, Autonoe and Agaue. During his reign he civilized the natives and in particular taught them to write 'Phoenician letters', in other words the North Semitic alphabet which is the parent of the Greek one (hence the practical identity of many of the letter-names in Greek, Hebrew and Arabic). The pitiful tales of Semele's affair with Zeus and of the sons of Agaue and Autonoe, respectively Pentheus and Aktaion, have been told (pp. 26, 53, 48). Ino (cf. p. 53) we shall meet again in the Argonautic saga. Later Kadmos and Harmonia went away to Illyria, where they were offered the leadership of the Encheleis (Eel-people) in accordance with an oracle. Having accepted this and conquered the Illyrians, Kadmos became their king and he and Harmonia were finally turned into serpents, in other words joined the semi-deified dead, for the serpent is a common manifestation of earth-powers. Indeed the whole story of the removal from Boiotia is to the same effect, for the land of the dead is regularly to the west, as Illyria is from Greece, and eels are etymologically and otherwise close akin to snakes in Greek language and thought.

Another start is made with king Labdakos, the later fortunes of whose dynasty are told in the next chapter. He died leaving an infant son, Laios, whose throne was usurped by Lykos, one of the Spartoi. His brother Nykteus had a daughter Antiope, who was loved by Zeus and took refuge from her father's anger in Sikyon, where Epopeus son of Poseidon married her. Nykteus killed himself in despair, but Lykos took up the task of punishing Antiope. He captured Sikyon, killed Epopeus and brought Antiope away. While on the journey back to Boiotia she brought forth twin boys, sons of Zeus, Zethos and Amphion. Grown to manhood, they met their mother, who had escaped from the prison in which Lykos and his wife Dirke had confined her. Learning who she was, they killed or at least deposed Lykos and tied Dirke to the horns of a bull. Her corpse was thrown into, or in some versions became the fountain which bore her name and was one of the principal water-supplies of historical Thebes. The brothers, having the kingship in their hands, now proceeded to build the walls of the city, most of the work being done by Amphion, who was so wonderful a musician that even stones would follow the sounds of his lyre and go where he would have them. Euripides used the twins in a once famous play, now lost save for some fragments, as symbols respectively of the practical man (Zethos) and the philosopher whose wisdom is justified in the end (Amphion). Amphion became the husband of Niobe (p. 46), and Zethos married Thebe, at least in some accounts, that is to say the city-founder and the city were closely associated, for Thebe is a pale figure with no myth of her own and several divergent accounts of her parentage, one of many who were called into being to 'explain' the name of some city or district.

Kalydon lies not far from Boiotia, and has at least one remarkable story. Oineus was anciently its king. His name clearly is connected with *oinos*, 'wine', and he was married to Althaia, 'healer', perhaps alluding to the medicinal use of wine. There is indeed an obscure story according to which Dionysos was Althaia's lover. The pair may well therefore have been originally local deities of viticulture. However, as we have them they are fully human. They had a son Meleagros and a daughter Deianeira, who afterwards became the wife of Herakles (p. 115). Oineus, when making a sacrifice to all the gods, forgot to include Artemis, and she sent a great boar to ravage his land. Meleagros collected a band of nobles from all parts to join in hunting the beast, and with them came Atalanta, a virgin huntress of whom quite divergent tales are told, for in some accounts she was an Arkadian, in others a Boiotian, and there are similar disagreements as to the name of the man who finally won her and the fashion of his wooing. Sometimes he is called Melanion, and he gained her affections simply by joining in her favourite pursuits and so getting to know and be known by her. Somtimes he is Hippomenes, and that is the name generally associated with her famous race. She had been exposed in infancy by her father, who wanted a son, and was suckled by a she-bear. When grown up, she was reunited with her parents but refused to marry any man who could not outrun her. As she was an excellent runner and the penalty for losing was death, this discouraged most suitors, but Hippomenes sought advice of Aphrodite, who provided him with three of the apples of the Hesperides (p. 110). These he threw in front of Atalanta from time to time, she stopped to pick them up, and he thus managed to win. Their son was that Parthenopaios (Girl-face) who took part in the expedition of the Seven (p. 118). But all this was later than the boar-hunt. Meleagros was much attracted by Atalanta, and when the boar, after great difficulty, was killed, he awarded its spoils to her, on the grounds that her spear had been the first to wound it. His mother's brothers objected strongly, the quarrel led to a fight and Meleagros killed them. His mother now took revenge by magical means. When Meleagros was born, she saw and heard the Moirai visiting the birth-room (as their present representatives, the Moires, are still thought to do) to settle the child's lot in life. One of them said that he should live until the log then on the hearth burned away. Althaia snatched it off the fire and preserved it preciously; she now burned it, and as it burned, Meleagros wasted and died.

This is the usual story, but Homer has a widely different one, with less flavour of *märchen* and more of normal heroic saga. The quarrel over the boar's spoils was between the Aitolians of Kalydon and the Kuretes, plainly a neighbouring people, not the attendants on the infant Zeus (p. 20). In the fighting a brother of Althaia was killed, apparently by Meleagros, and she formally cursed him, whereat he withdrew from the war and refused to take part until the Kuretes were actually storming the city, when at last he yielded to the entreaties of his wife Kleopatra, daughter of Idas and Marpessa (p. 46), and drove them off. He died sometime before the Trojan War, but Homer does not say how.

Somewhat farther north we come to Thessaly, which has some remarkable stories of its own. Ixion has some claim to be the first murderer, a Greek Cain. He married Dia, daughter of Eïoneus, and after the ancient manner was to pay a brideprice or bride-wealth to her father. But when Eïoneus came to claim it, Ixion contrived that he should fall into a pit of live coals and so perish. This, according to Pindar, was the first slaying of anyone belonging to the same *phyle* or tribe; it would seem therefore that Ixion and his wife's family were akin. No man would purify him from his blood-guilt, and at last he had recourse to Zeus, who received and cleansed him; presumably also he was fed on the immortal food and so could not die. He then proceeded to try and seduce Hera, and was beguiled by a cloud-phantom in her shape. He was bound to a wheel which revolves everlastingly, and the cloud-woman had a son who either was the first Centaur or became the father of the Centaurs, properly Kentauroi, a monstrous race half-horse and half-man, violent and lustful except for the wise and gentle Cheiron (p. 44). Besides their appearance in the adventures of Herakles (p. 111), they are noted for their war with the Lapithai; this seems to reflect a quarrel between a Thessalian people of prehistoric times and some wild mountain tribe whose enemies credited them with monstrous shape. The chief Lapith was Perithoos (Very swift), a son of Dia by Zeus, who married Hippodameia (not the heroine mentioned on p. 72) and had a son by her. The Centaurs were invited to either the wedding feast or, a less known form of the story, to the celebration of the child's birth, and either they became drunk, tried to carry off Hippodameia and the other women, and were defeated by the Lapiths, or there was but one Centaur present, Eurytion, who misbehaved himself, was cast out with loss of his nose and ears, and so began the quarrel. In the fighting Kaineus was killed. This Lapith had once been a girl, Kainis, who was raped by Poseidon, and offered any reward she liked. She asked to be made a man and thus safe against any such misfortune in future, and also for invulnerability. Hence the Centaurs were reduced to driving Kaineus into the earth with heavy blows, as they could not wound him.

Phthia, the kingdom of Achilles and his father Peleus, is in Thessaly, and it is curious that Peleus is represented as a son of Aiakos (p. 91) and his presence farther north accounted for by a story of manslaying; in one version, Aiakos had a bastard son Phokos (Seal-man) by a nymph, and the legitimate sons killed him and therefore were exiled. But Peleus' name certainly suggests a connexion with Mt Pelion. The then king of Phthia was called Akastos and had a wife Hippolyte, who behaved towards Peleus exactly as did Stheneboia towards Bellorophon (p. 78). Akastos contrived to steal a wonderful sword which Peleus had been given by Hephaistos, and to leave him asleep on Pelion, hoping that the wild beasts would devour him. But Cheiron gave him his sword again and he escaped; a fairly early form of the story gives the sequel one would expect, that he proceeded to overcome and take vengeance on Akastos and his treacherous queen.

Still in Thessaly, Kretheus, a brother of Salmoneus and Sisyphos (pp. 77, 149; they belonged to the numerous family of Aiolos, not the ruler of the winds whom Odysseus met, p. 142, but a son of Hellen, cf. p. 84, and eponymous ancestor of the Aiolian Greeks), had a son Pheres, father of Admetos (p. 45), whose other sons were Bias and Melampus. The latter saved the lives of some young serpents, and when they became mature they licked his ears as he lay asleep; on waking, he discovered that he could understand the speech of birds and other animals, whereby he became a famous diviner, for many creatures, birds especially, were credited with knowing more of the future than men. Bias wished to marry Pero, daughter of Neleus, the father of Nestor (p. 132), but Neleus would give her only on consideration of receiving the famous cattle of Iphiklos, a noble of the town of Phylake. These were guarded by a most formidable dog, and in attempting to steal them Melampus was caught and imprisoned. By listening to the conversation of woodworms, he learned that the room he was in would soon fall, and this forecast impressed Phylakos, father of Iphiklos, enough to make him inquire of the captive why Iphiklos had no children. This question was answered and a remedy prescribed, the cattle being the fee.

The rest of the Thessalian legends largely concern the Argonauts; but leaving Greece we come to Thrace, which contributes one very notable character to Greek story, Orpheus. This strange figure, musician, prophet, magician and priest of a new religion according to various accounts, had a wife Eurydike, a dryad, whom Aristaios (p. 45) tried to violate. Running away from him, she trod on a snake, and died of its bite. Orpheus determined to recover her, made his way into the lower world, and so charmed its inhabitants by his music that they let Eurydike follow him back to earth on condition that he did not look back at her on the way. He broke this tabu and she became a ghost again. This is the Greek, or Thracian, version of a story found in many countries, as far afield indeed as North America, whither it presumably came from Asia, of the man whose wife died and who went to the other world to get her back, regularly failing by some such disobedience as that of Orpheus. Having finally lost Eurydike, he would have nothing more to do with women, and met his death at their hands, for the Thracian Bacchantes fell upon him in the course of one of their orgies and tore him to pieces. His head, which was thrown into the Hebros, floated to Lesbos, where it spoke or sang, and gave rise to an oracle of Orpheus there.

This is not the place to discuss the large literature known as Orphic. From about the sixth century B.C. there were in circulation numerous works which, to judge by the quotations and references which are all we have left of them, were in the metre and style of Hesiod and dealt with cosmology and with doctrines of a theological and ethical nature, including some at least of the ideas of punishment, purification and reward in a future life mentioned on p. 59. It does not appear to be a true, as has often been asserted or implied, that there was a single consistent body of doctrine, still less that anything like an Orphic Church existed. It was rather the case that the age was one of speculation on religious and other matters, often crude in the extreme, yet including here and there ideas lofty enough to arouse the attention of such advanced thinkers as Plato. For some reason which escapes us, it was the fashion to attribute these works either to Orpheus himself, or to a relative or close companion of him.

If now we turn from the mainland to the islands, we may begin with two of the nearest, Salamis and Aigina. The latter was the home of Aiakos, son of Zeus and a nymph Aigina, daughter of the river Asopos in Boiotia. From her the island was said to have taken its name, having formerly been called Oinone. Aiakos was renowned for his justice, but his people were visited by a plague which killed them all. He showed his plight to Zeus, who performed a miracle; the inhabitants of an ant-hill turned into human beings, and so the island was repopulated. This story is associated with one of the worst puns which even ancient etymologists produced. 'Ant' in Greek is *myrmex,* and this word was pressed into service to explain the name of the people, the Myrmidons, over whom Peleus and afterwards Achilles ruled. This was not meant as a joke, although punning witticisms are common enough in Greek, for side by side with them ran the persistent feeling that a resemblance between two words was significant and might be an omen, for instance that the name of Pentheus (p. 53) was portentous, since it suggests *penthos,* grief or mourning.

Aiakos began the long connexion of his family with the saga of Troy. When Poseidon and Apollo undertook to build its walls for king Laomedon, they called Aiakos in to help them, and part of the fortifications was of his construction. When the work was done, three serpents suddenly appeared, and climbed the walls. Two of them fell dead, but the third ascended hissing triumphantly. It had chosen Aiakos' part of the building, and signified the place where the city was to be stormed, for the work of gods would naturally be impregnable to any human force. It was also explained to Aiakos by Apollo that his own offspring in the first and third generation should be at the taking of the city, which was fulfilled when Telamon his son helped Herakles to capture it (p. 112) and Neoptolemos his great-grandson saw its final sack (p. 137).

It has already been mentioned that his sons Peleus and Telamon left home (p. 89). The latter settled in the neighbouring island of Salamis, whence no doubt the Athenian interest in the whole family, for Salamis became an Athenian possession in the sixth century B.C., and therefore the

Athenians adopted the local hero-cults and their accompanying legends, to the extent, it was alleged, of interpolating a line into the *Iliad* (which seems to have been distributed largely by their copyists for some time), to the effect that Aias son of Telamon encamped near the Athenian contingent before Troy. Certainly Aias had a cult at Athens. Aias will be dealt with in connexion with the Troy-saga. His half-brother Teukros, son of Telamon by the captured Trojan princess Hesione (p. 112), was banished by his father when he returned without him, and going to Cyprus founded a city there which he named Salamis, after his native place.

Of the islands farther from Greece proper, Rhodes and Delos have already been mentioned (pp. 60, 40). The former was also the place of exile of the unfortunate Althaimenes, a Cretan of whom it was foretold that he should kill his own father, Katreus king of Crete. Going to Rhodes in order to avoid this, he murdered his sister Apemosyne, who had been violated by Hermes, supposing that she had misbehaved with a mere mortal lover. In the end, the prophecy was fulfilled, for Katreus, trying to visit his son, was taken by him for a brigand and so slain. Althaimenes, at his own prayer, was swallowed up in the earth, and later received a hero-cult. This tale is of uncertain date, for no early author attests it. Tenedos has a story which shows fairly plain signs of being an artificial legend; there was a demand for stories of the foundations of all manner of places, indeed it was hardly respectable not to have one. Tenedos claimed, then, at least in Hellenistic times, to have been founded by one Tenes, a native of Kolonai, who had had the same relations with his stepmother that Hippolytos (p. 83) had with his. His father, believing the woman's tale, set Tenes adrift in a chest, adding for some reason his sister Hemithea. They arrived in the island to which Tenes gave his name; the father, discovering the deceit, tried to be reconciled to his son, but Tenes rashly cut with an axe the mooring of his father's boat and sent him back. Hence 'Tenes' blow' became proverbial for a rash act. Tenes died defending his sister against Achilles' advances, and consequently, at the hero-shrine where he received the usual honours given to a founder, Achilles may not be mentioned and also no flute-player is admitted, for a flute-player gave perjured evidence to support Tenes' stepmother.

Delos, besides its connexions with Apollo and Artemis, once had a king Anios who was great-grandson of Dionysos and son of Apollo. By the favour of his divine ancestors he not only became a skilled diviner and priest of Apollo, but had three daughters, Oino, Spermo and Elaïs ('Wine-girl', Seed-girl and Oil-girl'), who could respectively produce wine, corn and oil at will. Again, no one before Hellenistic times testifies to this story, but it may of course be older. Another very pretty tale, doubtfully popular, was told by the famous Alexandrian poet, Kallimachos, and after him by Ovid and others. Kydippe of Keos was the lovely daughter of a rich and noble family. She was loved at sight by Akontios, who though of good family enough was poor and saw little chance of getting her parents' consent to marry her. Meeting her at a festival he threw her an apple, on which he had written 'I swear by Artemis to marry Akontios and no one else'. Picking the apple up, she read the words, pronouncing them aloud as was the usual ancient fashion in reading, even to oneself; Catholic priests preserve the custom when reading their breviaries. This was enough to bind her irrevocably; whenever her parents tried to marry her to another suitor, she fell extremely ill, and at last they perforce gave her to Akontios.

Cyprus has a story which, although found in no early author and of quite unknown origin and date, is so famous in modern times that it can hardly be omitted. A certain sculptor called Pygmalion (not a Greek name; the population of the island was a mixture of native Cypriote, Greek and Phoenician) was so disgusted with the loose lives of his fellow countrywomen that he would have nothing to do with them. He fell in love, however, with a beautiful female statue of his own making, and prayed to Aphrodite that he might have a wife like the statue. The goddess performed a miracle, the statue became a living woman, and Pygmalion married and had a son by her. Incidentally, the name Galatea by which many moderns call her has no ancient authority at all. Beyond this, the island yields little for the mythologist except the traditions concerning an ancient king, Kinyras, who was a favourite of Aphrodite. There may once have been a number of tales concerning him, but we have left little save the story of the birth of Adonis (p. 39). Apart from this there are mutually contradictory accounts of his parentage and his relationship to this and that royal house, Greek or foreign, and statements that he founded the cult of Aphrodite on the island, or the like.

Crete, as becomes its size and the antiquity of its culture, has a store of traditional tales. Agenor, king of Tyre, had a daughter Europê, who attracted the favour of Zeus. He took the form of a handsome and gentle bull, and playing about her as she walked on the seashore, at last induced her to mount on his back. He then plunged into the sea and carried her off to Crete. There she became the mother of three goodly sons, Minos, Rhadamanthys and Sarpedon. The mythical chronology is confused here, for Sarpedon is a hero of the Trojan War (p. 133), and not of prehistoric times, wherefore some omit him and some credit him with an amazingly long life. His presence in the tale may reflect real relations of Crete with the Asianic mainland, for he is regularly said to have been a Lykian. But the interest of the further legends centres around Minos, a word which yields no Greek meaning, but is very probably the Greek attempt at pronouncing a royal name or title of the Cretan dynasties. He became king of Crete, and one of his first acts, in some accounts the way in which he proved that the gods would do whatever he liked for him and therefore he was well fitted for kingship, was to ask Poseidon to send a bull from the sea, promising to sacrifice it. But when the animal appeared in answer to his prayer it was so magnificent that he kept it to breed from and sacrificed a more ordinary beast. Poseidon made the bull he had sent run mad, and worse still, Pasiphae, Minos' queen, conceived an unnatural passion for it. Now it happened that Daidalos of Athens was then a refugee in Crete. This man (his name means a skilful craftsman or artist) had murdered his nephew and pupil, who bade fair to outdo his own prodigious ability. Once again we meet a folktale, for this is the story known in English as the Prentice Pillar, telling of the learner whose natural abilities enabled him to excel his experienced and jealous master. Having thus incurred blood-guilt, Daidalos had fled from Attica, and was welcomed in Crete because of his artistic powers. Pasiphae induced him to help her, and by concealing her in a marvellously lifelike figure of a cow, he brought about the horrible union which she craved. She consequently bore a creature half-man, half-bull, known

generally as the Minotaur, i.e., *Mino tauros,* 'Minos' bull'.
Again Daidalos came to the rescue and built a maze, the
Labyrinth, in which the creature was placed. Here we catch
faint and uncertain echoes of genuine Cretan usages. One or
two bull-headed monsters, whether demons or masked
officiants in some rite, are shown in their art, and *labyrinthos*
is a word whose meaning we may plausibly guess as being
'place of the double axe', a sacred object in Minoan worship.
Minos himself has something superhuman about him, for
Homer informs us that he reigned for nine years and was the
'speech-mate of great Zeus', which might mean that he was
a priestly or even divine monarch whose powers had to be
renewed, or perhaps his person replaced by a younger man,
every nine years. Pasiphae, whose name means 'all-shining',
had a cult as a goddess in Lakonia, and their daughter Ariadne
(p. 82) has no small claim to have been likewise a goddess
originally. However, in the legends we have Minos is completely human. Daidalos wished to leave Crete, but either
because he set great store by his skill or to punish him for
pandering to Pasiphae's shameful passion, Minos detained
him, together with his son Ikaros. Daidalos, however, contrived a means of escape, by making wings of feathers stuck
together with wax, and on these he and Ikaros flew away
from the island. Ikaros soared too high, the wax melted in the
heat of the sun, and he fell and was drowned in that part of
the sea which was afterwards called Ikarian in memory of him.
Daidalos made his way to Sicily, and thither Minos pursued
him. King Kokalos protected the fugitive, however, and
when Minos arrived, the king's daughters, under pretence of
bathing him (a service occasionally done by a daughter of the
house to honoured guests, in Homer), killed him with boiling
water.

Another story of Minos is unconnected with Daidalos.
He had a son Glaukos, who was lost and could not be found
alive or dead. The Kuretes assured the king that whoever
could find the aptest simile for a remarkable tri-coloured cow
which he had would be able to restore the child alive. Polyidos,
an Argive seer, did best in this curious contest, which was a
not uncommon form of amusement in Greece, however
serious in this case; he said the cow was like the fruit of the
dog-rose. He then by divination found the body of the boy in

a large store-jar of honey, into which he had fallen and been suffocated. Minos now shut him up with the corpse, apparently in a tomb or similar place, and bade him bring Glaukos to life. Polyidos was quite at a loss, until he happened to kill a snake and saw another snake revive it by the use of a certain herb. Applying the same plant to the child he found it efficacious, and now the king demanded that Glaukos be taught divination. The seer complied, but before taking his final leave, he bade his pupil spit in his mouth. Having thus symbolically given back what he had received, Glaukos at once forgot all he had learned. The themes are familiar to all folklorists; animals of various sorts and not least serpents are commonly supposed to have great knowledge of virtuous herbs, and the final bit of symbolic magic is of a not unusual kind. We have therefore a popular tale, which need not originally have been told of Minos and Polyidos at all.

The mainland of Asia provides a tale or two, which as it happens are preserved only in late or comparatively late authors; Ovid is our best authority for both the following, practically the only authority for the first of them, which he tells as a story but little known. Pyramos and Thisbe (both are names of rivers) were young lovers in Babylon. Their houses were divided only by a party wall, and through a chink in this they communicated, for their parents would not hear of them marrying. They arranged to meet at the tomb of Ninos, the legendary founder of the city, and contrived to go there secretly, Thisbe arriving first. She saw a lioness and ran away from it, dropping her cloak, which the beast mouthed and so stained with blood, for it was fresh from a kill. Pyramos, coming a little later, found the cloak, supposed that Thisbe had been killed by the lioness, and stabbed himself; Thisbe, returning, found his body and killed herself with his sword. All this befell near a mulberry-tree, which was stained with the blood of the two, and consequently, though up till then mulberries had been white, they now are red. The other story is of a moral kind, teaching the virtue of hospitality. Zeus and Hermes disguised themselves, and went among mankind to test their charity. After being rudely repulsed by the rich, they found kindly entertainment from a poor old couple whose names, at least in Ovid, were Baucis and Philemon. Revealing themselves, the gods took their host and hostess to a mountain-top, whence they saw their impious neighbours destroyed by a flood. They then were granted a boon, to be priest and priestess of a temple into which their house had suddenly turned, and so lived for many years, finally being turned into trees. It is the Phrygian version, however Ovid got hold of it, of the widespread legend of the Flood.

When the Greeks colonized parts of Sicily and southern Italy, they naturally took some of their legends with them, and in particular located the scenes of many events in the *Odyssey* near their new homes. Into these identifications we need not go, for they are rather speculations than sagas. A few adaptions of Greek tales will be mentioned later; they come largely from Roman sources. Taras (Lat. Tarentum, the modern Taranto) had a foundation-legend involving the familiar theme of a fulfilled prophecy. Its legendary founder, Phalanthos, was long unsuccessful in finding a place to settle, till one day as he lay with his head in his wife's lap she wept for his misfortunes and her tears fell on his face. He then remembered that it had been foretold that he should found a city where he was rained upon from a 'clear sky'; and her name was Aithra, which has precisely that meaning. The prediction came true, and the city was duly founded. Kroton (Cortona) claimed no less a founder than Herakles (p. 110). One Lakinios, a brigand, tried to steal the cattle of Geryon from him, and in the ensuing fight Herakles accidentally killed his own host, a man named Kroton. He gave him honourable burial and foretold that a famous city should stand there. Siris, like several other places, claimed to have been founded by Trojan immigrants, and its cult-statue of Athena was said to have been brought by them. It had the appearance of having its eyes closed; probably the colour with which they were marked had faded with age. But the local explanation was that when the Ionians took the city they butchered certain persons who had taken refuge in the temple, and the goddess closed her eyes rather than look on such impiety. Temesa had its own curious association with Odysseus. One of his men had violated a girl there, and the townsfolk had killed him. His ghost troubled the land until a hero-cult was instituted in its honour and a girl given to it every year. This lasted till historical times, when Euthymos, a famous boxer, happened to visit the place, saw the intended victim, asked her if she would marry him if he overcame the ghost, and on her consenting, did battle with it. It was no phantom, but a figure material enough to be affected by Euthymos' fists, and it plunged into the sea and came no more. A picure which Pausanias saw attested the truth of the legend; the solid corpse-ghost is not without parellels in many popular traditions.

Siris, not content with its Trojan Athena, appropriated a tale of the death of Kalchas (p. 130) which really belongs to Klaros in Asia Minor. After the Trojan War, he met Mopsos and they had a contest of seer-craft; now it had been foretold that Kalchas would die when he met a better diviner than himself. He challenged Mopsos to say how many figs there were on a certain tree. Mopsos answered, correctly, that there were just ten thousand, and that they would precisely fill a bushel measure and leave one over. Kalchas thereupon died.

IV

CYCLES OF SAGA

The sagas discussed in the last chapter were mostly short and bound to some one place, generally a single city. There are a few more famous ones which, while they may have originated in a local tradition, have, so to speak, spread abroad, picking up incidents from various places and thus forming whole cycles and becoming known to the entire Greek world. To find one of these, we again start with the Argolid, the district which includes Argos itself, Mycenae and Tiryns, of which the first grew in relative and absolute importance in early historical times as the other two declined.

It is not a well-watered district; Homer's epithet for Argos is 'very thirsty' (*polydipsion*). Hence naturally its only river of any importance, the Inachos, has a prominent place in saga and myth. Inachos had a daughter Io, who was a priestess of Hera, the chief local deity, and attracted the notice of Zeus by her beauty. To hide his intrigue from Hera, the god changed her into a heifer, and himself approached her in the form of a bull. But Hera, suspecting the cheat, asked for the heifer, and Zeus could hardly refuse a gift apparently so trifling. She then set Argos to watch over the disguised Io; he is not a personification of the city, but a rather rare figure in Greek story, a monster with numerous eyes, who therefore was never fully asleep, for now one pair and now another could close and take rest. Zeus rid her of this intolerable guardian by the help of Hermes, who contrived to kill Argos, but Hera sent a fresh plague, a gadfly which drove Io away in wild flight from land to land. Exactly where she went is naturally a detail which varies with the geographical knowledge of the tellers of the story, but generally her wanderings include the Ionian Sea, supposed to have been named after her, and the Bosporos, interpreted as the Ford of the Cow, which she swam across

from Europe to Asia. Her ultimate goal, in all forms of the
story as we have it, was Egypt. There had been, besides
Mycenaean relations with that country, which were by no
means always friendly, a Greek settlement there since about
the seventh century B.C., Naukratis, a kind of treaty port, and
the Greek traders living or visiting there had opportunity to
learn something of Egyptian ways. Certainly they heard of so
famous a goddess as Isis, and seem to have confused her with
the cow-headed Hathor. The result was that Io and Isis were
identified. Io made her way to Egypt, where Zeus touched
her with his hand, thus restoring her to her human form and
her right wits, and she bore him a son Epaphos, interpreted as
'him of the touch' (*ephaptein,* 'to touch'). Again, this fitted Isis,
mother of Horus, at least to some extent. Now begins a curious
genealogy, made up of what Greeks at a fairly early date knew
of their neighbours in northern Africa and the Near East.
Epaphos grew and prospered, and begat Libye, i.e., Africa as
known to the Greeks of that time, the north coast and something of the hinterland. She in turn became the mother of
Belos, which, as it is the Hellenized form of Bel, a by-form of
Ba'al, links the genealogy with the Semitic-speaking peoples.
Belos also had children, and two of them bring the story back
once more to its geographical starting-point. One of his sons
was named Aigyptos, that is to say Egyptian, and another
Danaos, which practically means Greek, Danaoi being one of
the Homeric names for Greeks in general. Both had large
families, Aigyptos fifty sons and Danaos fifty daughters (the
number fifty is conventional in Greek, like forty in Hebrew; it
means hardly anything more definite than 'many'). The two
brothers quarelled, and Aigyptos proved the stronger. Danaos
therefore took flight with his family to Argos, where they
claimed Argive descent and sought the protection of the king
(Pelasgos, as some versions of the story name him; the word
signifies the pre-Hellenic inhabitants of Greece). Aigyptos
wished to marry his sons to Danaos' daughters, a perfectly
reasonable arrangement according to the law of various Greek
communities, including Athens, where a brotherless heiress
was married as matter of course to her nearest male kin. But
their cousins, fearing that marriage would mean nothing better
than enslavement to their own and their father's enemies
would not hear of it; Aeschylus indeed represents them as

filled with a hysterical aversion to marriage in general. Finally, the matter was settled by a pretended agreement to Aigyptos' terms. But by their father's directions, all but one of the daughters of Danaos killed their bridegrooms on the wedding night. The exception was Hypermestra, one of the two of that family who stand out as individuals from the undifferentiated remainder. She spared her husband Lynkeus and helped him to escape. Now the story becomes confused and is told variously in different authors; unfortunately we have but fragments of the oldest versions. But what seems to be the main tradition is that Hypermestra and Lynkeus were reunited and she bore a son, Abas, who was the father of a dynasty of Argive kings. Another sister, Amymone, was assailed by a satyr as she went to fetch water. Poseidon intervened, hurled his trident at the satyr, causing a spring of water to gush up where it fell, and enjoyed Amymone himself. It is pretty clear that she, whatever the origin of the other sisters, is a nymph of one of the local fountains. Concerning the remaining forty-eight, there is a quaint story at least as old as the fifth century B.C. Danaos offered them as prizes in a footrace; apparently the first runner to arrive had first choice of them and so on down to the last.

Attested by no early author but corresponding to quite early representations in art is a grimmer tale of what befell the Danaïdes (daughters of Danaos) after death. A fairly common punishment in the Greek hell, quite likely the product of Orphic imagination (p. 90) is the endless task of trying to fill a vessel with water, which can never be done because there is a great hole in it through which the water runs away as fast as it is poured in. Alternatively, the water has to be carried in a sieve or some such receptacle which cannot hold it. The sufferers from this kind of everlasting frustration are identified with the Danaïdes, though, as already said, not by any early author now extant. As usual, the crime and punishment are related. Water is needed for a lustral bath, and that is part of the ceremony of Greek marriage, which they profaned by murdering their husbands. Or it may be that it is wanted to purify them of blood-guilt, although the usual ceremony for that is to pour the blood of a victim, regularly a pig, over the sinner. In either case, they can never complete the rite.

Still in Argos and with characters genealogically connected with Danaos and his offspring, we meet another very famous story, that of Perseus. Abas (p. 101) had two sons, Proitos (p. 78) and Akrisios. The latter had a daughter Danaë, who was fated to bear a son who should kill his grandfather. To prevent this, Akrisios shut Danaë up in a tower of bronze, so that no man could come near her. But Zeus, who loved her, turned himself into a shower of gold and thus entering the tower got her with child. Akrisios put her and her baby son, whose name was Perseus, into a chest and set them afloat, an episode which occurs in a number of Greek legends, whatever its ultimate meaning may be. The chest came ashore on the island of Seriphos, and was hauled up in fishermen's nets. The king of the island, Polydektes, later fell in love with Danaë, but by that time Perseus was grown into a powerful young man, against whom Polydektes dared not employ open force. On an occasion when it was customary to make gifts to the king (this, in a stage of culture like that of Homeric monarchies, is a sort of equivalent of taxation), Perseus, who had no gift to bring, was cajoled into undertaking to fetch the head of Medusa the Gorgon (p. 31). As no one knew where the Gorgons lived, and Medusa had the power of turning anyone who looked at her to stone, this was a formidable task, but Athena favoured her half-brother and helped him with good advice. Guided by her and Hermes he made his way to the sisters of the Gorgons, the Graiai (p. 31), and stole from them their one tooth and one eye, which he refused to give back till they had told him how to reach certain nymphs who had the cap of darkness (or, as the Greeks called it, the helmet of Hades), the shoon of swiftness, the wearer of which could fly, and a certain wallet which, one may conjecture, was alone capable of holding so terrible a thing as Medusa's head; no surviving ancient gives any reason for its importance, and unfortunately we have only fragments of the earlier tellers of the tale. Being further provided by Hermes with a sword of adamant (a vague and mostly fabulous material, of extreme hardness; it has given modern languages their name for the diamond, the hardest of all substances), and getting their treasures from the nymphs (it seems· as we have the story, that he needed only to ask for them), he flew, still under divine guidance, to the stream of Ocean, where the Gorgons lived; with increasing geographical knowledge, the Greeks came to locate them in N.W. Africa, somewhere near the Atlas range. Now he approached Medusa, guided by her reflection, as she lay asleep, in a bronze shield, and cutting off her head, put it in the wallet. The other two Gorgons pursued him for a while, but lost him, as the cap made him invisible.

On the way home he approached the land of the Ethiopians; there he won a wife by rescuing Andromeda, daughter of Kepheus king of Ethiopia, from a sea-monster. Kepheus' wife Kassiopeia was a beautiful woman and had foolishly boasted that she was more beautiful than the Nereids, whereat Poseidon flooded the country and sent a sea-monster. Informed by the oracle of Ammon that the only way to get rid of this plague was to give the beast Andromeda to devour, Kepheus was forced to consent and she was bound to a rock to await it. At this moment Perseus arrived, saw and instantly loved Andromeda, won Kepheus' sworn consent to agree to their marriage if he rescued her, and duly overcame the beast, in some accounts by showing it the head of Medusa and turning it into a rock. He then had to encounter a certain Phineus, who had been betrothed to Andromeda previously and asserted his rights. He and his supporters were turned to stone, Perseus married Andromeda and stayed for a while with his father-in-law, and finally returning to Seriphos he rid Danaë of Polydektes' unwelcome attentions by using the Gorgon's head once more. He then left for Argos, having first given the kingship of Seriphos to Diktys, Polydektes' brother, who had been kind to Danaë. Now the prophecy was fulfilled, for though Perseus meant his grandfather no harm, an unlucky throw of a discus by him at some funeral games struck the old man on the head and killed him. Perseus continued to live in Greece, though not at Argos itself, and he and Andromeda became the ancestors of a line of kings.

That there is a strong element of folktale in all this is clear, and has often been remarked. That there was a dynasty, the Perseids, in the Argolid who traced their descent from the hero is perfectly possible, but does not amount to proof that any such person actually existed. Why he should be connected with so insignificant a place as Seriphos, which is a small island, and why his name, which yields no convincing Greek etymology, should suggest the Etruscan word *phersu,* signifying a sort of demon, are questions over which ingenuity and learning have been spent without, as yet, arriving at a universally accepted answer.

Still in the Argolid, we come now to the greatest and most popular of all heroes, Herakles of Tiryns. His name proves beyond reasonable doubt that whether real or imaginary he was from the beginning a man and not a god, for no Greek god has a theophoric name, that is to say one compound of the name of another deity, and Herakles means 'Hera's glory', i.e., probably 'glorious gift of Hera', a natural name enough in a population which had an ancient and famous cult of Hera and no doubt often prayed to her for children, but curiously inconsistent with her implacable hatred of him in the legend as we have it. It is perfectly possible that the original Herakles was a baron of Tiryns whose prowess in war and hunting made him famous, so that legend after legend accumulated about him; but in the nature of things this cannot be proved nor disproved. His story is complicated by Thebes claiming him as a native, or at least as having been born there of immigrant parents. In all probability there was a local strong man (again, he may have been real or imaginary) named Alkaios. The adjectival-ending -*ios* in the dialect of Boiotia often corresponds in meaning to the -*ides* of other forms of Greek, that is to say it forms a patronymic, a surname signifying 'son (or at least descendant) of So-and-So'. The result was that Herakles is quite often styled Alkeides, and duly provided with an ancestor whose name contains the element *alka-*, meaning valour or soldierly prowess. The genealogy is Perseus and Andromeda, Alkaios, Amphitryon. This Amphitryon was nephew to Elektryon, another son of Perseus and Andromeda, who became king of Mycenae and was involved in a war with the Teleboans, the inhabitants of the Echinades, which are islands off the west coast of central Greece. While helping Elektryon to drive home some cattle which the Teleboans had reived and he had recovered, Amphitryon hurled a throwing-stick at a reluctant cow and by pure mischance killed his uncle. This put blood-guilt upon him, and he left Mycenae for Thebes, taking with him Alkmene daughter of Elektryon. Elektryon had consented to her marriage with Amphitryon on condition that it should not be consummated till the Teleboans were defeated. The then king of Thebes, Kreon (another stopgap name, meaning merely 'king' or 'prince', cf. p. 75), purified him and consented to join in the war against the Teleboans, if Amphitryon would first help him to rid the country of the monstrous fox which plagued it (cf. p. 61). After conquering the Teleboans by Komaitho's treachery towards her father (p. 79), Amphitryon returned to Thebes. Zeus, however, had taken his form and anticipated him, and the result was that Alkmene conceived twins, Herakles son of Zeus and Iphikles (sometimes called Iphiklos) son of Amphitryon.

Herakles' adventures began literally in his cradle, for Hera in her jealousy tried to destroy him by sending a pair of huge serpents to the room where he and his twin lay. Herakles grasped one in either hand and strangled them, the first proof of his prodigious strength. Amphitryon, recognizing his supposed son as more than an ordinary child, had him carefully taught all manner of subjects, including of course wrestling and the use of weapons; for being a Greek hero he is not represented as overcoming his enemies by strength only, despite his superiority in this respect, but by skill also. He soon grew to manhood and after a few subsidiary adventures embarked on the great series of tasks, *athloi,* or as we commonly call them the Labours, which were imposed upon him by Eurystheus king of Mycenae, his kinsman. This brings him back to his native Argolid, and the reason for this servitude to Eurystheus was originally, there can be little doubt, the fact that the chief of Tiryns was subordinate to the lord of the more important Mycenae. But as we have the story, there was some less political cause, and one of the accounts connects the whole series of Labours with the saddest event of Herakles' life. Being happily married to Kreon's daughter Megara and father by her of several sons, he was driven mad by Hera and murdered his whole family. Behind this there seems to lie a Theban rite of offering to certain sons of Herakles; but as they are described by Pindar as warriors, and in the story of the madness they are young boys, clearly the whole tale has undergone much change in antiquity. In consequence, after being purified from the blood-guilt which automatically attached to him, the fact that he was not responsible for his actions being entirely irrelevant, he consulted the Delphic oracle as to where he was to live. The prophetess told him to live in Tiryns and perform the Labours, after which he should be made immortal. But the story of the madness told by Euripides in a famous play quite contradicts all this and makes it take place after the last of the Labours was done. Such inconsistencies and rival accounts are only to be expected when the saga is not one but put together out of many and embroidered by the imagination of countless known and unknown tellers from various parts of the Greek world.

However, be the reason for the Labours what it may, they are traditionally twelve in number, and fall into two groups, one within and one without the Peloponnese. The former are as follows:

(1) *The Nemean lion*. This formidable beast, which in most but not the earliest accounts was invulnerable, was ravaging the countryside about Nemea, the future site of the famous games. As we have the tale, Herakles battered it with his famous club (again, not the earliest form of this story, for he seems originally to have been thought of as armed like a normal Greek infantryman), and then strangled it in his arms, got its hide off (a quaint detail in one account is that only its claws would pierce the skin and Herakles had to haggle it off by using them) and thenceforth wore it as a cloak.

(2) *The Lernean hydra*. This was, as its name implies, a formidable water-snake; Lerna is a marshy district. It had several heads, and if one of them was destroyed, another, or two more, grew in its place; or one of them was immortal. To make matters worse, the hydra had an ally in the shape of a huge crab, which attacked Herakles' foot. He managed to kill the crab, and bade his nephew Iolaos, son of Iphikles and his faithful comrade, to bring firebrands, with which he seared the hydra's necks as the heads were destroyed, and so prevented any new ones from growing. Herakles was thus able to kill it, buried the immortal head under a heavy stone, and dipped his arrows in the creature's gall, which was extremely poisonous. Here we probably have a genuinely old detail, for in the Homeric tradition, arrow-poison is not used except by the unorthodox Odysseus, and archery had declined in historical times and was little thought of by the classical armies. Even Homer does not know how the formidable composite bows employed by a few of his characters were made; perhaps the art had been already lost in his day. The

immortal head seems to be a local tradition, for in later times the spot where it was buried was supposedly known.

(3) *The hind of Keryneia.* In the surviving lists of Labours, this and the next are sometimes transposed. We do not know how old the list is nor who drew it up, but it somehow became, so to speak, canonical, with but slight variants in the main events, though details differ from author to author. But all agree that the hind was a remarkable creature. Although female, it had antlers, and sundry other supernatural features, such as bronze hooves, are credited to it by one writer or another. At all events, it was sacred to Artemis, and so might not be hurt. Herakles pursued it, but the extent of the chase is a little consistent as the wanderings of Io (p. 99); like them, it varies with the geographical learning of the teller, or his fondness for bringing in mentions of strange lands. He caught it at last (in some versions he was reproached by Artemis in person, but excused himself by pointing out that he was merely executing Eurystheus' orders), brought it to Mycenae, showed it and let it go.

(4) *The boar of Erymanthos.* This sounds like a duller doublet of the last adventure; the boar was not sacred, and there is no reason given why Herakles should not have simply hunted and killed it. However, he was ordered to bring it in alive, and therefore tired it by chasing it into deep snow, where he netted it and brought it to Eurystheus on his shoulders. This was rather a favourite subject of the earlier vase-painters, who often show Herakles bringing the creature to his taskmaster, who cowers in a great bronze jar, said to have been his regular refuge against the hero, of whom he was mortally afraid.

(5) *The birds of Stymphalos.* The thick woods around a lake at Stymphalos in Arkadia were full of birds which for some reason (there is no agreement as to what it was) were objectionable and their extermination therefore to be desired. Herakles frightened them from their cover with the noise of a bronze rattle, made either by himself or by Hephaistos, and shot them on the wing.

(6) *The stables of Augeas.* Augeas, or Augeias, was son of Helios and king of Elis. He was very rich in cattle, and his byres had never been cleaned. Herakles contrived to do so in one day; it is usually said that he turned a river, the Alpheios or another, through them. For the sequel, see p. 112.

The remaining Labours are extra-Peloponnesian. They are:

(7) *The Cretan bull.* This was either the bull loved by Pasiphae (p. 94) or the one (in this version, clearly not Zeus in disguise) which had brought Europê to the island (p. 94). Like the hind and the boar, it was simply caught by Herakles, brought to show to Eurystheus, and then let go. It made its way to Marathon, where Theseus disposed of it (p. 82).

(8) *The horses of Diomedes.* This Diomedes had nothing to do with the son of Tydeus (p. 134), but was king of the Bistonians, a Thracian people. His horses were fed on human flesh, and in what seems to be a later form of the story, anxious to tone down the marvels, Herakles resorted to the services of a volunteer army to overcome them and their master. Diomedes was killed in battle, or captured by Herakles and fed to his own horses, which thereupon became tame and tractable and were brought back and dedicated to Hera at Argos.

(9) *The Amazon's girdle.* Hippolyte, queen of the Amazons (p. 78), had a girdle which, perhaps because it possessed magical powers of some kind, was much to be desired. Again Herakles is said sometimes to have gone alone and sometimes to have collected an army (Theseus shared in the exploit by Athenian accounts), and either he killed Hippolyte and took the girdle from her corpse, or Melanippe, her general, was captured and the girdle demanded as her ransom. In any case, it was brought back and dedicated in the temple of Argive Hera, where in later days it was shown to visitors. It is one of many objects, some at least no doubt really old, which were to be found in such places and had an explanatory tale attached to them.

It will be remembered that Herakles in one account at least was promised immortality at the end of the Labours. The remaining three are variants on that theme; in all of them he triumphs over a power of the extreme west (the quarter of sunset and therefore of death) or actually of the other world. There is an older tale, not included in the canonical list, but known to Homer and mentioned by Pindar. Herakles on some occasion fought and defeated Hades in person, 'at the Gate, among the dead'.

(10) *The cattle of Geryon.* Geryon, or Geryoneus, was a triple-bodied or three-headed monster living on Ervtheie, i, e.,

Red Island, coloured presumably by the beams of the setting sun, and located farther and farther west of any places inhabited by Greeks till finally it was placed somewhere in or off Spain. He possessed large and very fine herds of cattle, guarded not only by himself but by his dog Orthros and his herdsman Eurytion. The dog was no common beast, but the offspring of Typhon (p. 21) and Geryon's sister Echidna, another monstrous creature, half woman and half (what her name signifies) serpent. Her brood further included Kerberos, the hydra of Lerna, the Chimaira (p. 78) and the Sphinx (p. 117). Geryon himself is probably not a demon or god of the world of the dead, but one of what may be called the upper layer of chthonian or underground powers, possessors and on occasion givers of fertility, both vegetable and animal. It is very doubtful if his name is Greek. Certainly the cattle have nothing ghostly about them. Herakles succeeded in killing Geryon and his attendants, and then drove the cattle away. Here, as in the case of the hind (p. 107), we get large geographical developments, since all manner of places, especially Greek settlements westward of the mother country, were anxious to have some connexion with so famous a hero. On the way to Erytheie Herakles passed through what is now the south of France, and there the natives, who were Ligyes (Ligurians) set upon him. He kept them off with his bow till his arrows were spent, and then prayed to Zeus for help. Zeus responded by raining down large stones, with which Herakles pelted his foes till they were put to flight. The return, according to an early account, was comparatively easy. Herakles got hold of the great golden cup in which the Sun nightly makes his way back from west to east to be ready for his next rising, and in this he and the cattle sailed the stream of Ocean without further incident. The getting of the cup entailed some violence, for Herakles threatened either Helios or Okeanos with his bow. But the better-known versions take him back by a route which can be approximately followed on a map. He crossed the Pyrenees and the Alps with his booty and went down through Italy to the Straits of Messina, across which he swam the cattle and so reached Sicily. How he got from there to Greece is nowhere clearly explained; in other words, what interested the tellers of this form of the tale was to connect him somehow with the

Greek colonies in Sicily and the south of Italy (Magna Graecia). The Roman adaptation of the legend will be told later (p. 161); that part of it which concerns Kroton has already been mentioned (p. 97). In Sicily, he met Eryx, king of the mountain and town which bear his name, and son either of Poseidon or of Aphrodite (i.e., the region lies on the sea-coast, and there was a famous shrine of the goddess there). Eryx challenged him to wrestle, or to box, Herakles accepted and killed him. Much more remarkable, yet probably springing from a like source, the desire of Greek settlements to have some sort of connexion with the hero, is his appearance in the east, where he seems to replace some native Scythian hero or god. In this form of the tale, Geryon's island is somewhere about the Euxine (Black Sea), and Herakles has some horses, which wander away. He asks a monstrous creature, part woman and part serpent, if she has seen them, and she asks for his embraces as the price of telling him. He consents, and she bears three sons, Agathyrsos, Gelonos and Skythes, of whom the last, when he grows up, is able to draw a bow of Herakles and put on his girdle; he therefore becomes king of the country, and the other two, driven away by their mother, become the originators of two peoples, the Agathyrsoi and Gelonoi. This may serve as an example of the way in which non-Greek tales were drawn into the cycle of the legend of Herakles; the normal versions all take him to the west, where the Pillars of Herakles, marking the Straits of Gibraltar, testified to his farthest point and became proverbial for the utmost limits of human endeavour.

(11) *The apples of the Hesperides*. Again the order is a little uncertain, for this and the next Labour are sometimes interchanged. The Hesperides (p. 87) kept a wonderful garden somewhere in the far west, in which golden apples grew. As becomes such fairy-like creatures, they were and are hard to locate, although the commonest account puts them in Libya (N. Africa), somewhere not far from the Atlas range. Herakles, after some subsidiary adventures, was directed to inquire of Nereus (p. 30), who was unwilling to tell him, and, after the fashion of sea-creatures, took all manner of shapes till finally Herakles managed to bind him and force the secret from him. Arrived at the garden, he overcame the dragon which guarded the place, got the apples, and brought

them back. But they did not remain among men, for Athena took them away, as being too sacred to leave their own place permanently.

(12) *Kerberos.* The most formidable task of all was to bring up Hades' hound from the lower world. As might be expected, the fancy of various tellers of the story played around it, and national vanity took a part; for instance, the Athenians said Herakles took the precaution of being initiated in the Eleusinian mysteries before risking himself among the dead. Like Odysseus (p. 143), he met some celebrated ghosts, including Meleagros (p. 87), the brother of his future wife Deianeira, also Theseus and Perithoos, who had descended in an impious attempt to steal away Persephone for Perithoos to marry. Hades had caught them and they were seated, unable to rise. As usually said, Herakles wrenched Theseus loose, but could not rescue Perithoos. But he managed to capture Kerberos, showed him to Eurystheus, and let him go back again.

The Labours form the kernel of the saga of Herakles, but his other adventures are too numerous to be told in full. Ancient mythographers classified them as *parerga,* or works incidental to the Labours, and *praxeis,* actions independent of them. A few of the best known of the former were the following. When going after the boar of Erymanthos, Herakles was hospitably entertained by Pholos, a Centaur who was not of the race of Ixion but a son of Seilenos (p. 32) and a nymph. When asked for wine, Pholos was reluctant to open the store-jar which was the common property of the Centaurs, but was prevailed upon to do so; whereat the others, attracted by the smell, invaded Pholos' cave and were driven off and some of them killed by Herakles. Pursuing them, he came upon Cheiron (p. 88), who also was of better stock than the rest, being son of Kronos and the nymph of the lime-tree, Philyra, with whom the god mated in stallion-shape, having changed her into a mare to disguise her from Rhea. Cheiron was accidentally wounded by one of Herakles' poisoned arrows, but being immortal could not end his pain by dying, till at last, at least in some versions of the story, his immortality was transferred to Prometheus (p. 24), who had by that time made his peace with Zeus. Pholos handled another arrow, accidentally wounded himself with it and so died. When Herakles cleansed the stables of Augeas, he had been promised a tenth of the cattle as his reward (to vow a tithe to Herakles was in historical times quite common among those embarking on some enterprise), but cheated of it on the feeble plea that it was really the river and not he that did the work. Herakles then came against Elis with an army, but had great difficulty, owing to Augeas' formidable allies, the Molione ('two sons of Molione'), a pair of identical twins (perhaps 'Siamese' originally), children of Poseidon and a certain Molione wife of Aktor, Augeas' brother. However, he contrived to kill them both, took Elis, killed Augeas and made his son Phyleus, who had sided with him, king in his place. To celebrate his victory, he founded the most famous of the Great Games, those at Olympia, near Elis, in honour of his father Zeus. Henceforth the festival was held every four years in late summer and consisted of sacrifices in honour of Zeus and other deities and a progressively more elaborate programme of sports, the prizes for which had no money value, but consisted of garlands cut from a wild olive-tree. When and by whom the games were really founded is unknown.

It was while on his way to encounter Diomedes that Herakles wrestled with Death to save Alkestis (p. 45). While returning from the expedition against the Amazons, he touched at Troy, and there found its king Laomedon in sore distress. When Poseidon and Apollo (p. 91) built the walls for him, he cheated them of their pay, and Poseidon sent a sea-monster, Apollo a plague. The monster, oracles assured Laomedon, could be appeased only if his own daughter Hesione were given it to eat, and he consequently exposed her on the shore. At this moment Herakles arrived and promised to save her if he were given the king's famous stud of horses which he had received from Zeus when Ganymedes (p. 156) was carried off. With great difficulty, Herakles killed the monster, which in one version of the story swallowed him and had to be dispatched from within. Then Laomedon refused to keep his part of the bargain, and Herakles in due season collected an army, which included Telamon (cf. p. 92), took the city, handed over Hesione to Telamon as his slave-concubine, and spared a son of Laomedon, Priam, to be king over what was left of his father's realm.

On his way to the Hesperides he had two noteworthy encounters. A giant, Antaios by name, insisted on wrestling with him; being a son of Earth, Antaios was refreshed every time he was thrown by contact with his mother, so Herakles was obliged to dispose of him by lifting him clear of the ground and crushing him to death. Atlas, some say, actually got the golden apples for him, Herakles meantime supporting the sky. On returning, Atlas proposed to leave Herakles to his prodigious task, but was somehow beguiled or forced into resuming it himself. On that Labour or some other occasion he found himself in Egypt, where an evil king, by name Busiris (this much at least is genuine Egyptian, for it is a corruption of Per-Usire, 'house of Osiris', a city in the Delta), sacrificed all strangers to Zeus (presumably Re or Amon-Rê), having been assured that this was the best manner of averting drought (as if Egypt ever had any noticeable rainfall). Herakles resisted him and his followers and soon made an end of them. What set this curious tale going we do not know; Herodotos rightly points out that such sacrifices are quite contrary to all real Egyptian custom. Many other minor exploits, serious for the most part but often comic, are credited to him; to tell them all would be wearisomely lengthy for anyone not a specialist.

More important are the *praxeis,* which include his greatest service to the gods. It had been foretold that they could not overcome the giants (p. 21) unless a mortal fought on their side, and Herakles was the inevitable choice. As we have the story, it was on this occasion that he slew Alkyoneus, a rather vague figure concerning whom we have but brief and contradictory accounts; but they agree that Herakles killed him somewhere and sometime. The place of the contest is usually said to be Phlegrai or Phlegra, but sometimes Pallene, a peninsula running out from Chalkidike into the Thracian Sea. Phlegra itself is rather inclined to wander, for its name was attached to the Phlegraean Fields in Italy, a volcanic region not far from Naples. We can roughly date this part of Herakles' saga, for the Gigantomachy, or battle of the gods and giants, cannot be traced further back than about 575 B.C. either in literature or art, although mentions of giants are much earlier, but Herakles' part in the struggle is familiar to Pindar, who refers to it in odes written about a hundred years later than that date. Herakles therefore seems to have had this addition made to his adventures in the sixth century. It is not often that we can thus catch a mythological story in process of growth.

Herakles is regularly shown as amorous and also as a great eater, characteristics of the strong man in popular imagination. The latter trait is prominent in two stories, one at least of which is an *aition* of a strange rite at Lindos in Rhodes, where the sacrifice to Herakles was accompanied with formal and ceremonial cursing, for some reason as unknown to us as to the ancients. But the tale which professed to explain it was that Herakles, being hungry, helped himself to a plough-ox, killed it and ate it whole, while the unfortunate ploughman could only curse him. Theiodamas king of the Dryopes was served in like manner, but being a king he retorted much more vigorously; a battle ensued in which Theiodamas was killed and Herakles took his young son Hylas to be his page and favourite.

Besides innumerable casual amours, Herakles is represented as having married twice, and the second marriage and its preliminaries led to complicated results, the fruit of his story having in some cases quite obviously become entangled with alien saga or myth. He had a passion for Iole, daughter of Eurytos, king of Oichalia in Euboia, but her father and most of her brothers objected, either because they were afraid he might go mad again and murder a second wife and her children, or for some other reason. The quarrel with Eurytos and his sons was made worse by Herakles later on killing one of them by treachery, the only time he was guilty of anything worse than open force. Once more there was blood-guilt upon him, and he sought purification from Neleus, king of Pylos (Navarino), who refused it him. Later he appealed to Delphoi, but Apollo would give him no answer until Herakles caught up the holy tripod on which the priestess sat to give her inspired oracles and started to carry it off. Herakles and Apollo were stopped from actual combat by Zeus, who hurled a thunderbolt between them, and then Apollo gave an answer, that Herakles must be sold as a slave for a time. His purchaser was a foreign princess, Omphale, queen of Lydia; in other words, here the Greek hero becomes confused with the consort of one of the many Oriental mother-goddesses, who is regularly inferior to her. His term of servitude completed, he was free to seek revenge on Eurytos.

Another search for a wife had better success. At some time before or after falling in love with Iole, he visited the kingdom of Oineus (p. 87) and paid court to his daughter Deianeira. She had another suitor, the river-god Acheloos, and the two fought, Herakles defeating his opponent, who was in the form of a bull, and breaking off one of his horns. He then married Deianeira and started for home with her, his dwelling-place at that time being Trachis, near Mt Oite. On the way they had to cross a river, and the Centaur Nessos carried Deianeira across, as it was his custom to do for any who chose to pay him. On the way, however, he tried to violate her, and Herakles, hearing her cry for help, shot the Centaur. Dying, he assured Deianeira that the blood from his wound would act as a potent love-charm and prevent Herakles from preferring any other woman to her. She therefore collected some of it and kept it by her.

Herakles embarked on a number of campaigns, the last of which led to his death, or rather his apotheosis. He sought revenge on Neleus, and killed him and all his sons except one, Nestor, who succeded his father and was still alive at the time of the Trojan War (p. 132). He also made a campaign against Sparta, whose king Hippokoon and his sons had sided with Neleus, and again was successful, although his brother Iphikles was killed in the fighting. Finally he set out against Eurytos, took and destroyed Oichalia and carried off Iole. By this time he and Deianeira had been married for a number of years and their eldest son Hyllos had reached manhood. Deianeira, learning of her husband's possession of Iole (who as we have the story was much younger than she; the chronology, as might be expected, is very confused), thought it proper to use Nessos' charm, and put the blood on a new garment which she sent to him. But Nessos had deceived her; being mixed with the venom of the hydra (p. 106), the blood was a deadly poison, and Herakles was soon seized with intolerable pains. He gave orders that he should be carried up into Mt Oite and burned on a great pile of wood. This consumed his mortal parts, and he passed to his place among the gods, having Hebe (p. 25) for his consort. Here again we can trace the origin of the story. There was an ancient fire-rite on the mountain, at which, besides animal sacrifices, little human effigies were thrown into a great fire, thus furnishing an explanation of the whole ceremony; it had become some-how connected with Herakles (who originally has nothing to do with that part of Greece), it made a sort of pretence of burning men, therefore Herakles had been burned there.

Herakles' children formed a sort of connecting link between him and the Dorians, who seem to have had no great legendary hero of their own, and also wanted some kind of justification for their conquest of the Peloponnesos; in the Archaic period and for long after a mythological claim was taken seriously. They therefore declared that in consequence of some help which Herakles had given to their king Aigimios in a war with the Lapithai (p. 88), Aigimios had adopted Hyllos and made him heir to part of his kingdom. Thus the Dorian migration and their resultant conquest of parts of Greece were mythically the Return of the Children of Herakles (*Herakleidai*). But they had long to wait before their 'return'. First they were persecuted by Eurystheus, and having no other protector than Iolaos, now old and feeble, sought refuge, according to the Athenian story, at Marathon, where they were kindly received by king Demophon, son of Theseus. Eurystheus prepared to invade Attica, and victory could be bought only by the sacrifice of a virgin of noble birth. Makaria, Herakles' daughter, offered herself, battle was joined, and old Iolaos by miracle was for one day restored to the vigour of his prime. Eurystheus was killed, either by Hyllos in the battle or after it, when he had been taken prisoner by Iolaos and brought to the aged Alkmene, who insisted on his being slaughtered.

Eurystheus being dead, Herakles' heirs had a sound claim to his kingdom, for Herakles, like Eurystheus, was of the stock of Perseus. Accordingly they made for the Peloponnesos, but were advised at Delphoi to await the third harvest before attempting to enter. Hyllos, the eldest son, took this literally, and three years later attempted to invade, but was defeated and killed by the Peloponnesians under Tisamenos, son of Orestes. A further consultation of Delphoi led to the explana-tion that 'third harvest' meant the third generation, and in due season a second attempt was made, this time with success, after sundry incidental adventures and mishaps. The Pelo-ponnesos was divided between the three leading men of Herakles' stock, Temenos getting the Argolid when they cast lots, Prokles and Eurysthenes, as representatives of their dead father Aristodemos, Sparta, and Kresphontes, Messenia. This among other things accounted for the fact that Dorian Sparta always had two kings reigning simultaneously. Kresphontes did not reign long, being assassinated by a pretender, Poly-phontes; but his young son Aipytos was smuggled out of the country, and when he came to manhood made his way back and avenged his father; the story is familiar enough to anyone who has read Matthew Arnold, for it is the subject of his dramatic poem *Merope,* founded ultimately on what we know of the plot of Euripides' tragedy of the same name.

Moving now into central Greece, we come to the tragic history of the House of Labdakos at Thebes. The young Laios (p. 86), hospitably received by Pelops and grown to manhood in his house, ungratefully kidnapped his son Chrysippos. This brought a curse upon him, and he was warned by Apollo that if he begat a son by his wife (Epikaste in Homer, Iokaste in later writers), that son would kill him and marry his own mother. He and Iokaste had a son, whom Laios at once exposed on Mt Kithairon, thrusting a spike through the baby's feet, presumably to disable his ghost. But the child was found by a shepherd of the childless Polybos, king of Corinth, and given to Polybos, who adopted him. Grown to manhood, Oidipus (Swell-foot), as he was named, was taunted with being no true son of the royal house. He went to Delphoi to inquire concerning his parentage, and was told that he was fated to kill his father and marry his mother. Assuming that Polybos and his wife were really his parents, he resolved never to return to Corinth. On the way from Delphoi he was met by Laios, quarrelled with him and killed him. He then went to Thebes, which was in sore distress, for a monster, Phix in the local speech, Sphinx in the mouths of most Greeks, had taken up her quarters near Thebes and asked a riddle of all passers-by. If they could not guess it, she killed them, and had in this manner destroyed many. Oidipus guessed the riddle, which is said to have been to the following effect: 'There is a creature which goes sometimes on four legs, sometimes on three and sometimes on two, and the more legs it has, the weaker it is'. He replied. 'Man crawls on all fours in babyhood, walks on two legs when full grown, and hobbles with a staff when old'. The Sphinx then killed

117

herself; another tradition, preserved in art only, was that Oidipus overcame and killed her in flight. At all events, Kreon (cf. p. 105), who was governing Thebes now that Laios was dead presented the deliverer with the kingdom and the hand of the widowed queen. Oidipus unsuspectingly married Iokaste (the women of Greek saga seem to remain young and attractive at a comparatively advanced age), and they had two sons, Eteokles and Polyneikes (Truly-glorious and Much-contentious), also, at least in the later versions of the tale, two daughters, Antigone and Ismene. But a plague fell on the city; the oracle bade them discover and expel the slayer of Laios, and Oidipus, making determined efforts to do so, found out the whole truth. Iokaste killed herself; Oidipus, in Homer, continued to be king, ultimately falling in battle, but in later tellings of the tale blinded himself, or was blinded, and either went at once into exile or remainded in seclusion; the former is the better-known story, and linked with an Attic legend according to which he ultimately vanished from among men at Kolonos, near Athens, the holy spot where he entered the underworld being known only to king Theseus and his successors. The latter is, however, the earlier and continues the story better. Eteokles and Polyneikes neglected their father, and especially did not set before him that cut of meat which was esteemed the best and therefore a king's prerogative, whereupon he cursed them, saying that as they did not know how to divide the meat, they should not know how to divide the kingdom. So it befell, for they came to an agreement to rule in alternative years, but Eteokles, who had the first period of sovranty, would not give up the throne to Polyneikes. But the latter, going into temporary exile when his brother became king, had taken refuge in Argos, and there met with Tydeus, a son, legitimate or otherwise, of Oineus (p. 87), who had been obliged to leave home because he had killed a man in a quarrel. The two exiles were recognized by Adrastos, king of Argos, as the boar and lion to whom an oracle had bidden him give his two daughters, for one had a boar, the other a lion, on his shield, or they wore cloaks made from the hides of those beasts. Accordingly, they were married and Polyneikes now claimed the help of his father-in-law to recover his rights. Tydeus joined in the enterprise, and Adrastos enlisted the help of four or five other notable chiefs,

Kapaneus and Hippomedon from Argos itself, Parthenopaios (cf. p. 87) from Arkadia, Amphiaraos the great seer, who foreknew the ill success of the undertaking, but was over-persuaded into going by his wife Eriphyle, she having been bribed by Polyneikes with the necklace which Harmonia (p. 85) had been given on her wedding-day. Generally a fifth name, that of the rather obscure Eteoklos, is added, Adrastos being represented as taking no active part in the fighting. When he is shown as one of the champions, this name is naturally dropped. Tydeus went to Thebes to try and arrange a peaceful settlement, but had no success; furthermore, he was ambushed on the way back by fifty Thebans, of whom he killed forty-nine, sparing one to take the news home. The Argive army now set out. On the way they passed through Nemea, and there met Hypsipyle (p. 124), who had been captured by pirates and sold as a slave to Eurydike, wife of Lykurgos, the local king. At Amphiaraos' request, she showed them where to find water, and in guiding them left on the ground Opheltes, the baby son of Eurydike, whose nurse she was. On her return she found that the child had been devoured by a dragon. The Argives killed the beast, protected Hypsipyle from the vengeance of her mistress, and buried Opheltes, whose funeral games (a common feature of the elaborate funerals of princes in heroic times) were the first celebration of the Great Games of Nemea, held henceforth in alternate years (in reality, they were of no importance till 573 B.C.). Shortly afterwards, Hypsipyle was met, recognized and taken away by her sons. Opheltes, whom Amphiaraos re-named Archemoros ('beginner of death') as being the first casualty occasioned by the expedition, is in all probability a minor but very ancient child-god of a well-known Cretan type.

Reaching Thebes, the seven champions assailed its seven gates, which were defended by a like number of chosen Thebans. The defenders were completely successful. Of the Argives, Amphiaraos was swallowed up alive in the earth as he retreated, and henceforth continued his prophetic career by giving oracles from underground. Kapaneus was destroyed by a thunderbolt as he mounted the walls, defying even Zeus to keep him out. Polyneikes, meeting his brother, killed and was killed by him. The rest fell fighting except Adrastos, who whether an actual combatant or not got away safely, thanks

to his wonderful horse Areion, the offspring of Poseidon by
Demeter, who had taken the shape of a mare to avoid his
attentions, and was approached by him in the guise of a stal-
lion.

The next generation saw the defeat turned into victory.
The sons of the seven chieftains made in their turn a more
successful attack upon Thebes, which they took at last without
resistance, the survivors of its garrison and people having
secretly retired by the advice of the prophet Teiresias. Of the
Argive leaders one only, Aigialeus, son of Adrastos, fell in the
fighting; Adrastos himself, now a very old man, died of grief
on the way home.

The House of Labdakos thus came to an end, though there
was at least one family, the Emmenidai, to whom Theron,
the famous tyrant of Akragas (Agrigentum) in Sicily belonged, who claimed descent from it through Thersandros,
son of Polyneikes. It remains to mention the fates of two or
three subordinate figures in the story. Chief of these is undoubtedly Teiresias, who is famous from Homer on for his
prophetic powers. He is credited with two extraordinary
adventures. One was, that he saw two snakes coupling and
stepped on them or struck them with his staff, whereupon he
changed from a man to a woman, and so remained till he saw
another pair so engaged, treated them in the same way, and
was restored to his original sex. He is regularly said to have
been blind in later life, and two tales professed to account for
this. One was, that Zeus and Hera asked him, since he alone
had been of both sexes, to determine which of them had more
pleasure of love-making, and on hearing that the female had,
Hera angrily struck him and deprived him of sight. The other
version is that he, somewhat like Aktaion, had the misfortune
to see a goddess bathing, in this case Athena, who was the
friend of his mother Chariklo. More merciful than Artemis,
she did not kill him, but blinded him only, compensating
him with the gift of prophecy, a staff which magically guided
him, and long life. He met his end during the evacuation of
Thebes, after drinking of the waters of the spring Tilphussa.

During the first siege, Teiresias declared that the city
could be saved only if one of the Spartoi (p. 85) sacrificed
himself to the ghost of the sacred dragon. Menoikeus, Kreon's
son, volunteered for this duty, stabbed himself on the walls

120

and fell into the ancient lair of the monster. After the defeat of the Argives, Kreon decreed that their bodies, or at all events that of Polyneikes, should be refused burial. Antigone (p. 118) set this edict at defiance, and managed to give Polyneikes a formal interment by throwing dust over his corpse. Being caught, she was shut up in a tomb by Kreon and left to starve, but anticipated this by hanging herself. Her betrothed, Haimon, son of Kreon, killed himself over her body. That is Sophokles' telling of the story, but Euripedes has a longer more romantic version, in which she was rescued, and married secretly to Haimon, and bore him a son, who years afterwards was recognized by a birthmark in the shape of a spear which all the Spartoi had. The loss of the play and the muddled state of accounts which seem to go back to it make it doubtful how the story ended; it is equally doubtful if it is due to anything more than the poet's own imagination, for he often took liberties with traditional tales. By Athenian accounts, Theseus (p. 82) persuaded or compelled Kreon to allow the burial of the dead.

On Alkmeon or Alkmaion, son of Amphiaraos, devolved the duty of avenging his father's death on Eriphyle (cf. p. 73). He duly killed her and, like Orestes, was haunted by the Erinyes. After a number of minor adventures (some again due perhaps to nothing more than Euripedes' fancy and told in plays of his now lost) he settled on an island newly formed by the silt of the river Acheloos, for he could find rest only on ground upon which the sun had not shone at the time of the matricide. Here he ended his days, married to Kallirhoe, daughter of the river-god. A subsidiary tale makes him die by assassination, the result of a quarrel with the family of a former wife of his, and be avenged by Kallirhoe's infant sons, miraculously grown at once to manhood. The fact seems to be that our surviving accounts of him are a confused blend of several distinct stories.

The story of the Argonauts is in many ways a puzzle, including the question of its original location. On the one hand, the heroes concerned are commonly called Minyai and alleged, in direct contradiction to the names and homelands of most of them, to be descendants of Minyas, the legendary king of Orchomenos (or Erchomenos) in Boiotia. On the other, their voyage starts from and returns to Thessaly, and Thessalian names are prominent in the legend. Perhaps the best explanation of at least some of these difficulties is that our form of the tale took shape at Miletos, which claimed to have as its founder one of the family of Neleus (p. 114), a house which in turn claimed descent from Minyas. This would at all events account for the prominence of the Euxine (Black Sea) in the narrative and the location of the Land (Aia), to which they went, at the far end of it, at Kolchis on the river Phasis. Miletos traded in that direction. The main outlines are as follows.

(1) *Preliminary*. Athamas (p. 53) was married to Nephele (Cloud), who bore him two children, Phrixos and Helle, and then mysteriously disappeared. Ino was his second wife, and hated her step-children. In order to get rid of them she beguiled the women into roasting the seed-corn and when Delphoi was consulted concerning the resulting famine, she bribed the messengers to bring back word that Phrixos, in some accounts Helle also, were to be sacrificed. Now Nephele intervened and brought her children a marvellous gold-fleeced ram, on whose back they were carried overseas towards Kolchis, Helle falling off on the way at the straits thenceforth called the Hellespont (the Dardanelles) after her. Phrixos was kindly received by Aietes (Man of the Land), who had been warned to do so; he was a son of Helios and had two daughters Chalkiope and Medeia, and a son Apsyrtos. Phrixos in time married Chalkiope and had four sons by her, and later died peacefully in his father-in-law's city. The ram had been sacrificed to Zeus Phyxios (Zeus of the Flight) and its fleece hung up in a grove guarded by a sleepless dragon. All this is more *märchen* than saga.

(2) *The beginning of the quest*. Kretheus, brother of Athamas and son of Aiolos (p. 80), was king of Iolkos in Thessaly, and died leaving a son Aison and a stepson Pelias, the latter the child of his wife Tyro by Poseidon and twin brother to Neleus. Aison, as Kretheus' legitimate son, naturally succeeded him, but Pelias by one means or another deposed him, or contrived to succeed on his death. Aison had a young son Jason (properly Iason or Ieson according to dialect), who was sent away out of Pelias' reach by his parents, or his mother, and entrusted to Cheiron (p. 88). When he reached early manhood he set out for Iolkos to claim his rights. Either he

wore one shoe only because that was the Magnesian fashion of dress (shoe for walking over sharp stones, bare foot to get a better grip on mud), or he had lost one in fording a rain-swollen river. In one version, which is obvious folktale, he had carried across a poor old woman who, once he reached the other side, revealed herself as Hera in disguise and promised to favour him for his courtesy. Pelias on the other hand had gained her disfavour. As we have the story, he had neglected to sacrifice to her when offering to the other gods (cf. p. 87), but to parallel the incident of Jason and the supposed old woman, he should have refused her help when in her humble disguise. At all events, he had been warned by an oracle to beware of the one-sandalled man, and also that he was doomed to destruction by one of the line of Aiolos. He therefore met Jason with a plausible tale that the ghost of Phrixos haunted him in dreams, demanding that the golden fleece be brought back. Jason readily agreed to attempt this, and assembled a number of heroes (over fifty in all), including several who had special gifts of one sort or another, as Zetes and Kalaïs, the sons of the North Wind, who could fly, Argos the skilled craftsman, who by Athena's help built the first fifty-oared warship, the Argo, Lynkeus, who had preternaturally keen sight, Tiphys, who was an accomplished pilot, and others; though as the tale is told in our authors they tend to merge into the usual Homeric pattern of warlike nobles, and their special gifts are made little use of. The lists differ greatly in different sources, but regularly include the fathers of the men who fought before Troy, or some of them, and veterans of the Kalydonian boarhunt, (cf. p. 87). Manifest intruders are Herakles and the Thracian Orpheus, of whom the former is soon got rid of, the latter is not heard of till the sixth century B.C., and so is badly out of place in a legend older than Homer. That behind it all there lies a real adventure of enterprising seafarers, whether in the direction of the Euxine or elsewhere, is probable enough, but the original facts are buried deep under accretions of fancy.

(3) *The Voyage.* As with Io (p. 99) and Herakles (p. 107), the accounts vary with the geographical knowledge of the tellers, also with different ideas of how the Argonauts got back when their quest was achieved. Briefly, and omitting many details, there were three versions. (*a*) After reaching

the Land, wherever it was, they were near enough to the ends of the earth to get into the stream of Ocean and sail around till they could reach familiar seas and make their way to Iolkos. (*b*) They simply came back the way they had gone. (*c*) They penetrated into Central Europe by going up the Istros (Danube) and then either made their way into the North Sea, presumably down the Rhine, and so around the British Isles and down the west coast of Europe to the Straits of Gibraltar, or else followed some mysterious and largely imaginary river system which ultimately brought them out somewhere in the western Mediterranean. Generally, (*b*) seems to have been unpopular, as it left fewer places and fewer adventures to diversify the narrative, and (*c*) in its second form is in a way the standard account, followed by the best-known ancient telling of the story, the *Argonautica* of the Alexandrian poet, Apollonios of Rhodes. (*a*) however left its mark even on him, for he contrives (by a convenient storm which drives the Argo off her course as she is nearing Greece) to get them to Africa, where it seems they found themselves in (*a*) after quitting Ocean. I follow Apollonios in the main, as being the earliest complete account surviving; but variants are innumerable, and would take a larger book than this to give even a brief account of.

Sailing from Pagasai, the nearest port to Iolkos, the Argonauts made their way up the coast to the island of Lemnos. Here there were no men but only women, for recently the women had incurred the displeasure of Aphrodite, who had made them all repulsive to their husbands. The men therefore had quitted them and got themselves Thracian concubines from the nearby coast. In reprisal, the women had killed all the men on the island, only Hypsipyle, the daughter of their king Thoas, son of Dionysos, sparing her father and getting him secretly out of the country. The Lemnian women now welcomed the Argonauts, who mated with them and stayed in Lemnos for some time. In particular, Jason mated with Hypsipyle, who conceived twin sons by him. Going on at last, they reached the peninsula afterwards known as Kyzikos, where its eponym, the local king, received them hospitably. They in turn delivered him from the Gegeneis, a sort of giants who were infesting the country, Herakles with his archery taking a prominent part. But on their departure they met bad weather, and were driven back to Kyzikos' territory in the night. The inhabitants, supposing they were raiders, set upon them, and in the fighting Kyzikos was killed. The Argonauts, when morning came, found his body and gave it honourable burial. His wife Kleite wept bitterly for him and hanged herself. Her tears turned into the fountain which in future bore her name. The bad weather continued, and Mopsos, the prophet of the expedition, advised propitiatory rites in honour of the Mother of the Gods. These being performed, the storm ceased and the Argo went on. Rowing in the still disturbed water, Herakles broke his oar with a too vigorous stroke, and they landed to spend the night and get material for another. Hylas (p. 114) went to fetch water for their supper, and came upon a fountain inhabited by Naiads, who were so attracted by his beauty that they pulled him in to live with them. Herakles sought long and vainly for him and at last the ship left without him.

They next halted in the land of the Bebrykes, a savage people of Bithynia, whose king Amykos demanded that one of them should box with him as the price of getting water from the local spring. Polydeukes (p. 74) took up the challenge and knocked Amykos out by his superior skill, though the latter was much the larger and heavier. The Bebrykes then attacked the Argonauts, but were beaten off with heavy loss. Next they approached the Bosporos and visited old Phineus, who was dragging out a miserable existence in punishment for a sin which he had committed; accounts differ as to what it was. He had lost his sight and in addition the Harpies (p. 30) haunted his table, stealing most of the food and defiling the rest, so that he was nearly dead of hunger. The Argonauts agreed to rid him of this plague, if he would advise them as to their future journey. When the Harpies swooped down, Zetes and Kalaïs rose on their wings and pursued them through the air till they were bidden by Iris to quit the attempt, in return for a solemn assurance that Phineus should no longer be molested by them. The point at which they turned back was over the islands known thenceforth as the Strophades, interpreted as Islands of Turning. Phineus now told them that they would shortly come to the Kyaneai (Black rocks) or Symplegades (Clashing rocks), at the entrance to the Euxine, which were constantly in motion, drifting apart and then clashing together. They were to let a dove loose as they came near them, and if the dove passed between them unhurt, the ship would do likewise. Furthermore, they were to seek the favour of Aphrodite, for the issue of their enterprise lay in her hands. Taking his advice, they saw that the dove had got through with the loss of a few tail-feathers caught by the rocks as they came together. Rowing their hardest, they just managed to pass with slight damage to their sternpost, by the secret help of Athena. The rocks now became motionless, as they were fated to do if ever a ship got between them safely; so at least the story is told by Apollonios, but Homer knows nothing of this detail (cf. p. 143).

This was their chief adventure on the way to Kolchis, although they passed by many lands of strange peoples, but coming near to their goal they picked up the sons of Phrixos and Chalkiope, who had set out to visit their father's country and been shipwrecked. They were a welcome reinforcement, for one of the original Argonauts, Idmon, had been killed by a wild boar and Tiphys had died, the ship being now steered by Ankaios, a son of Poseidon. They came to the mouth of the Phasis, rowed some way upstream and put into the bank, concealing their ship in a reed-bed. Meantime, at the urgent request, according to Apollonios, of Hera and Athena, Aphrodite inspired Medeia, Aietes' younger daughter, with intense love for Jason. Here we pass once more into *märchen*, for this is the well-known story generally known in English as Ogre's Daughter, in which the hero, being set impossible tasks by some formidable person who has him in his power, is helped to perform them by his taskmaster's daughter; we shall meet the same tale again with the sexes reversed on p. 147; Medeia was a skilled witch, and a priestess of the witches' goddess Hekate. Aietes, on being approached by the Argonauts, first abused them roundly for pirates, and then becoming a little more reasonable bade them produce someone who could perform the following exploit. He had a pair of bronze bulls, the work of Hephaistos, which breathed fire. These were to be yoked to a plough and an assigned portion of land ploughed. Next, the ground was to be sown with some of the teeth of Kadmos' dragon (p. 85), and the armed men when they sprang up were to be defeated and destroyed. Jason volunteered, without much hope of success, but Medeia met him secretly and gave him, besides good advice, a magic ointment which he was to rub with due ceremonial on his body and armour. The effect would be to make him invulnerable to weapons and to fire for a day. He did as she advised, and in the presence of Aietes and his people forced the bulls, by sheer strength, to the plough, being unhurt by their fiery breath, ploughed and sowed the field, and then used Kadmos' stratagem of throwing a stone at one of the warriors, which started a fight among them resulting in the death of them all. He now claimed the fleece, but Aietes put him off to the next day, planning to fall upon and kill all the Argonauts during the night. Medeia, guessing this and fearing also for her own safety, collected her most potent charms, escaped early in the night from the palace, and went on board the Argo. They went down-river to the grove, where she lulled the dragon to sleep or killed it and Jason seized the fleece. They then set off for home, but were pursued by Aietes' men. Here the story varies. In one account, Aietes himself led the pursuit, but Medeia had brought with her her brother Apsyrtos, who in this form of the tale was a young boy. She murdered him, cut him in pieces, and strewed the severed limbs in the wake of the ship. Aietes, stopping to pick them up, was thus delayed. It seems likely that here, as in the stories of Theseus and Atalanta (pp. 82, 87), we have once more a folktale, the familiar magic flight in which objects of magical potency are thrown in the way of a pursuer. The other version smacks less of folklore. In it, Apsyrtos was a grown man, and commanded the pursuers. He caught up with the Argonauts, and while Medeia beguiled him with a pretence of parleying, Jason treacherously set on and killed him. His men were afraid to return to Kolchis with their mission unfulfilled, and scattering in various directions, founded sundry settlements here and there. But the blood-guilt rested on Jason, until coming to the island of Kirke (p. 143), he underwent an elaborate ceremony of purification at her hands. The rest of the return is a series of unconnected adventures, some of them resulting from a desire to bring the Argonauts to various sites said to be Minyan, perhaps with a measure of truth, for it seems likely that the Minyai, whoever they were, had a real existence and were a seafaring people.

Arriving at last at Iolkos, their next business was to dispose of Pelias, who in some accounts had taken advantage of Jason's absence to murder Aison, and in any case is regularly represented as a treacherous rascal. Medeia told his daughters that she could make the old young, and to prove it, cut an old ram, boiled him in a cauldron with certain magic herbs, and produced him transformed into a young lamb. In another variant, the subject of the crucial experiment was Aison himself, who had not been murdered but was simply living in retirement. Sometimes both Aison and the ram are rejuvenated. In any case, the daughters of Pelias were convinced, cut up their aged father and put him in the cauldron, but this time Medeia provided them with herbs of no efficacy, and thus put upon them the guilt of patricide. Akastos, son of Pelias, drove her and Jason out of the country and celebrated his father's funeral with games of great magnificence, which formed a favourite subject for some of the earlier poets. Now their story becomes obscure, for it is caught up in the Corinthian tradition. Taking refuge in that city, Medeia lost her children, whom she took one by one as they were born to the temple of Hera, expecting for some reason that they would become immortal. Another story is that they were murdered by the Corinthians, and their ghosts caused much trouble till they were appeased by honorific rites; and yet a third, famous from Euripedes' use, perhaps invention, of it is that she killed them herself to spite Jason, who intended to quit her and marry the daughter of the local king. At all events, she left Corinth and took refuge in Athens (cf. p. 81). Jason, according again to Euripedes, met an appropriate end. He had dedicated the Argo to Poseidon at his shrine on the Isthmus of Corinth, and one day as he sat under it some of the fabric fell on him and killed him.

Lastly we come to the most famous of all saga-cycles, that of Troy. Here we need have no doubt that the story has a historical foundation; there was a settlement near the Dardanelles of people having an Achaian culture, and we may well believe, as tradition tells us, that they were both wealthy and warlike, also that they had a tinge of Asiatic civilization, shown in the double names, one Greek and the other foreign, which some of them bear (Priam is said to have been called Podarkes originally, Paris his son has another name,

Alexandros, Kassandra his daughter is also Alexandra) and also in the description of the kings as having children by many women, in other words of having a harem of Oriental fashion. But the facts concerning this cultural outpost of the Mycenaeans, as it almost certainly was, and the quarrel between it and the Greeks of the mainland under their war-leader Agamemnon, are too thickly overspread with legendary details for more than the barest outline of them to be made out at present. Here is the story as we have it.

Like Goethe's *Faust*, it has a prologue in heaven. Earth complained to Zeus that men were too numerous and too overweening, and he determined on a war to lessen their numbers and pride. Priam (Priamos) king of Ilion (Troy) had as his chief wife, Hekabe (Hecuba in Latin and generally in modern languages). Being with child, she dreamed that she bore a firebrand, consequently when her child Paris was born, Priam exposed him. But he was rescued by shepherds, came to manhood, and revealed himself by his strength and valour, overcoming his brothers in various contests. Thus he was recognized and reunited to his family, despite the warnings of Kassandra, who was as usual disbelieved (p. 46). In Homer, he had offended Hera and Athena by railing on them when they visited him on some unspecified occasion, and praising a third person, very likely Aphrodite, who gave him the dangerous gift of *machlosyne,* female sexual desire, in other words the power to make any woman he chose desire him. Later authors have a more elaborate story. When the gods were at the wedding of Peleus and Thetis (p. 63), Strife (Eris) threw a golden apple among them inscribed 'For the fairest'. Hera, Athena and Aphrodite all claimed it, and to settle the matter Paris, who was the handsomest of mankind, was appointed to judge between them. All three offered him bribes, power, success in war, the loveliest of women for his wife. The last attracted him most, and he awarded the apple to Aphrodite, thus incurring the undying enmity of the other two goddesses, of whom Athena was one of the principal deities of his own city. Shortly afterwards he took ship for Greece, visited Menelaos' palace and in his absence seduced and eloped with Helen (cf. p. 75). Agamemnon called together the other suitors of Helen and an expedition against Troy was set on foot. In fact, it seems probable that the

Achaians of that date had a loose central organization, at least for warlike purposes, with the king of Mycenae at the head of it.

The preliminaries to the war lasted long, as long as the war itself in most accounts. Unsuccessful negotiations were entered into with the Trojans, who were influenced by Paris to refuse to return either Helen or the treasure she had taken with her. Of the chieftains who had sworn to support Helen's husband, Odysseus, king of Ithake (the modern Thiaki, not far from Corfú), was reluctant to go and pretended to be mad; but Palamedes, his rival in cleverness, reputedly the inventor of the alphabet, detected him. Odysseus was ploughing in an assumedly mad fashion, but Palamedes set his young son Telemachos in the way of the plough, and Odysseus showed his sanity by turning out of the furrow to avoid hurting the child. Assembled at their rendezvous, Aulis on the Boiotian coast opposite Euboia, they were stayed by contrary winds, and Kalchas the prophet revealed to Agamemnon that Artemis demanded the sacrifice of his daughter Iphigeneia. He consented reluctantly, and either the sacrifice was performed or Iphigeneia was rescued at the last moment by Artemis and a hind substituted for her, while she was conveyed miraculously to the land of the barbarous Tauroi and became priestess of the goddess there. Why Artemis was angry is a question variously answered. Agamemnon had vowed to sacrifice to her the fairest creature that should be born in his domains in a certain year, and that was Iphigeneia. Or he had unwittingly killed a deer which was sacred to Artemis, or on killing an ordinary stag had said that not even the goddess could have shot more truly. All these explanations are plainly secondary additions to the story. Setting out at last, the expedition took a wrong direction and landed in Mysia, where Telephos (p. 77) resisted their invasion. In the fighting, Achilles, son of Peleus and Thetis, the most noteworthy of the chieftains, wounded him, and the wound would not heal. After the Achaians had left the country, he was advised at Delphoi that only the inflictor of the wound could cure him, and therefore disguised himself as a beggar, made his way to the Greek camp, contrived by one means or another to get a hearing, and was met with Achilles' protest that he was not a physician. Odysseus, however, guessed rightly that the spear

which had wounded Telephos was meant, and the application
of rust from it cured the wound. On the way to Troy, the
leader of one of the contingents from north-eastern Greece,
Philoktetes, son of Poias, was lost to the expedition. Poias had
lit Herakles' pyre (p. 115), and been given the hero's bow and
arrows as his reward; these had descended to his son. During a
sacrifice to a minor deity, Chryse, Philoktetes was bitten in
the foot by a snake, and the wound, though not fatal, was
loathsome and at times so painful that Philoktetes disturbed
all his comrades with his cries. He therefore was left ashore on
Lemnos and remained there till towards the end of the war.
Helenos, a Trojan seer taken prisoner by the Greeks, revealed
the secret that Troy could be taken only by the arrows of
Herakles, and therefore Odysseus and Diomedes went to
Lemnos and induced him to come with them. Machaon, son
of Asklepios (p. 44), healed the wound, and Philoktetes
shot Paris with one of Herakles' arrows. He might have
been cured if his deserted mistress, the nymph Oinone, who
was skilled in medicine, had not refused her aid, out of offence
at his infidelity. When he died, she killed herself from remorse.

The course of the war was a long process of blockade and
attrition, not a siege in any proper sense, for the tactics of
that day were still very elementary. The Achaians under
Agamemnon encamped on the shore of the Hellespont (Dardanelles), thus cutting the Trojans off from the sea, and
fought them as opportunity arose, meanwhile taking, one by
one, the smaller places in the neighbourhood, which were
weak enough to be captured by storm. Several combatants
on both sides stood out from the rest. Achilles (Achilleus),
son of Peleus and Thetis (p. 63) was by common consent
the foremost among the assailants, by reason of his valour,
strength, beauty and swiftness; the story that he was invuler-
able through having been dipped in the Styx by his mother
in infancy, and therefore could be wounded only in one foot
by which she had held him, has no early authority and is
contradicted by his being slightly wounded in the shoulder by
a quite insignificant enemy in Homer. Next to him came
Aias (Ajax), son of Telamon (p. 92), a man of unflinching
courage and enormous strength, but slow-witted. A lesser
namesake of his was the son of Oileus, a Lokrian, courageous
and nimble but of unpleasant character. Diomedes, son of

Tydeus (p. 118), had all his father's valour, and a less furious temper; indeed he is almost the hero of the *Iliad*, prominent in fighting and ready with good advice in emergencies. Athena favoured him as she formerly had his father, whom she would have made immortal if he had not disgusted her by gnawing the head of his fallen enemy Melanippos while he lay dying. Palamedes, who seems to be an intruder into the tale of Troy, is got rid of by an act of base treachery on the part of Odysseus, whose character steadily degenerates in the post-Homeric tradition. Odysseus had never forgiven him for forcing him to go with the expedition, and forged a letter from Priam to him which if genuine would have been clear evidence of a plot to betray his comrades to the Trojans. The false charge was believed and Palamedes stoned. Odysseus himself is prominent not so much in fighting, though he displays both courage and skill on occasion, as for his cunning, which shows itself in various ruses and daring enterprises (as when he made his way into Troy itself in disguise and came back with useful information), and his wise advice. Prominent in council, though his advice is generally quite futile, is old Nestor, son of Neleus (p. 115), a man of about seventy according to Homer; he had seen two generations, and was still king in the third, a generation being some thirty years. He shows himself at the front, but never is seen actually fighting, for which he no longer has the strength or agility. Outstanding among the Trojans are especially two sons of Priam, Paris and Hektor. The latter, who has no non-Greek name (*hektor* means approximately 'sustainer'), is possibly Homer's own invention. He is second only to Achilles as a warrior, and of lofty and noble character, patriotic yet desirous of a reasonable peace, a loving husband to his wife Andromache and proud of his little son Astyanax. Being also a prudent man, he foresees that in time Troy must fall, but meanwhile does his utmost to prevent or at least delay the catastrophe. Paris, who is somewhat backward in fighting, distinguishes himself principally as a dangerous archer; here he has a counterpart on the Achaian side, Teukros, the bastard son of Telamon by Hesione (p. 112), who fights valiantly at the side of his half-brother Aias. The junior branch of the Trojan royal house was represented by Aineias, better known to moderns under the Latinized form of his name, Aeneas, son of Anchises and Aphrodite (the genealogy probably goes back to some myth of the local mother-goddess and her inferior but divine consort), who was destined to survive the war and rule the remnant of the Trojans; for the greater fortune which Roman mythologists found for him, see p. 161. Of the elders of Troy, a notable figure was Antenor, who from the first was in favour of surrendering Helen and all her property and thus avoiding or ending the war. Knowing this, the victorious Achaians spared him and his family, and after the war he made his way to Italy and founded, so the Roman tradition at least had it, the city of Patavium in the valley of the Po. Of the numerous allies who came to the support of Priam from various quarters, the most outstanding were the Lykian contingent, and of these the chieftains, Sarpedon, son of Zeus (cf. p. 94) and Glaukos, a descendant of Bellerophon (p. 78), were the most noteworthy.

The first nine years of the war were comparatively obscure and the interest heightens, for us and the ancients, in the tenth and last, and that not solely because the plot of the *Iliad* is taken from events of that time. Agamemnon had had assigned to him Chryseis, i.e., the girl from Chryse, a town in the Troad, whose father Chryses was priest of Apollo. Her name, corrupted to Cressida, furnishes the heroine of one of the most celebrated mediaeval continuations of the Troy-saga, made especially famous by Chaucer's and Shakespeare's handling of it. Chryses offered to ransom his daughter, and was roughly repulsed by Agamemnon; he prayed to Apollo to avenge him, and a plague soon forced Agamemnon into sending Chryseis back and making sacrifice to the offended god. But he insisted on being recompensed, and therefore seized a captive belonging to Achilles, Briseis ('the girl from Brisa', another local town). Achilles thereupon withdrew himself and his followers, the Myrmidons, from the fighting, and his mother Thetis induced Zeus to give victory to the Trojans till her son was sufficiently avenged. Zeus sent a deceitful dream to Agamemnon, assuring him that he would immediately take Troy. He therefore led out his army to battle. Hektor proposed to settle the matter by a duel between Paris and Menelaos, the victor to take Helen, and a truce was agreed to on those terms. Menelaos won, but before he could kill Paris, Aphrodite saved him and brought him to Helen's

133

bedchamber. Then Athena, bent on the destruction of Troy, persuaded Pandaros, one of the Trojan chiefs, to break the truce by shooting an arrow at Menelaos, who was slightly wounded by it. Fighting began at once. Several of the Achaians did valiantly, especially Diomedes, who defeated Aineias and took his horses, and then, encouraged by Athena, drew blood from Aphrodite herself as she was carrying her son out of danger, and went on to wound Ares, who had joined in the fight on the Trojan side. He met Glaukos, but on discovering that there was a hereditary friendship between their families, they separated peaceably, exchanging Diomedes' plain bronze armour for Glaukos' splendid golden equipment. Aias son of Telamon accepted a challenge from Hektor to single combat, and had rather the better of it; but on the whole the battle was indecisive. Now, as Homer clearly realizes, though some of his commentators do not, Priam could afford this better than Agamemnon, for the latter's strategic reserve, such as it was, was on the other side of the Aegean, while Priam could, while his great wealth held out, hire contingents of allies from the hinterland and so make good his losses. The Achaians therefore forfeited their camp, which had hitherto consisted merely of their ships drawn up on the beach and some huts built on the landward side of them, and Agamemnon was extremely discouraged. By Nestor's advice he sent an embassy to Achilles, offering not only the return of Briseis, untouched, but a huge payment (in kind; there was as yet no coined money circulating), by way of honour-price. Achilles, hitherto manifestly in the right, put himself in the wrong by scornfully rejecting the offer, and Agamemnon now hoped for nothing better than to hold off attacks until he could get his men aboard their ships and withdraw. During the night, however, he was encouraged by a small success. The Trojans were encamped on the plain; Odysseus and Diomedes volunteered to scout towards their lines, and find out what they intended doing. They captured a Trojan scout, Dolon, and learned from him the whereabouts of a newly arrived Thracian contingent, whose leader, Rhesos, they contrived to kill as he slept, together with some of his followers, and capture his magnificent chariot-horses, which they rode back to camp. Thus cheered, Agamemnon confidently resumed the battle the next day, but after long and arduous fighting was wounded and his army driven back on its fortifications. Then, as Sarpedon and afterwards Hektor broke through the wall, Achilles relented so far as to dress Patroklos, his dearest friend, in his own armour and let him lead out the Myrmidons. The intervention was quite successful, and the Trojans driven back to their city, Sarpedon falling to Patroklos; but Patroklos, pressing his victory too far, was first repulsed from the wall of Troy by Apollo in person, then stunned by a blow from the god, wounded by a minor chieftain, Euphorbos, and finally killed by Hektor, who stripped off his armour and put it on himself. The rest of the Greeks had much difficulty in carrying off Patroklos' body and were forced back to their camp again. Achilles, after a wild outburst of grief, was reconciled to Agamemnon, accepted his offer, and next day but one set out against the Trojans, whom he had already kept out of the camp by merely appearing at the ditch before the wall and shouting his war-cry. Hektor, with much less than his usual prudence, had again bivouacked in the open, and the Trojans were utterly routed and driven with heavy loss back to the shelter of their walls. Thetis, seeing her son left without any armour which he could use, had got him new and magnificent equipment from Hephaistos, and this he wore in what was to be almost his last great fight, for it had been foretold to him by his mother that he would die soon after Hektor. The latter was ashamed to enter Troy, and awaited Achilles outside the gate. At the last moment his nerve gave way and he ran from his enemy three times around the walls, helped to a last burst of speed by Apollo. He was halted, however, by Athena, who took the shape of Hektor's brother Deïphobos and pretended to have come to his help. When she disappeared he knew that that was the end, rushed to close quarters with Achilles and was fatally wounded, living long enough to ask that his body be not maltreated and, when that was denied him, warning Achilles of his own doom. Achilles dragged his corpse at the tail of his chariot back to the camp; after elaborate mourning Patroklos was buried and funeral games held, and for twelve days Achilles dragged Hektor's corpse daily around his friend's tomb. It was, however, preserved by the gods from decay and mutilation, and Priam, encouraged by a message from Zeus and guided by Hermes, made his way by night to Achilles' quarters, ransomed his son's body and took it back to Troy; its burial ends the *Iliad*.

The authors of what is known as the Epic Cycle continued the story. Two important reinforcements reached Troy, first a party of Amazons led by their queen Penthesileia, and afterwards an Ethiopian army under Memnon, son of Tithonos and Eos (p. 61). Both these leaders were killed by Achilles, who shortly afterwards met his own death at the hands either of Paris aided by Apollo or of Apollo himself disguised as Paris. He was shot in the foot by an arrow, obviously poisoned, for the wound was quickly fatal, and his body brought back to the Achaian lines by the greater Aias, after heavy fighting, to be buried with due honours amid the wailing of Thetis and her fellow-Nereids. His place as leader of the Myrmidons was taken by his son Pyrrhos or Neoptolemos (Red-head or Young warrior). At the first rumour of the war, Thetis had disguised Achilles as a girl and hidden him among the daughters of king Lykomedes, ruler of the island of Skyros. There he had an affair with one of them, Deidameia, who bore him a son, by this time come to manhood (the chronology is clearly vague, for Achilles himself is represented as quite young when he died), and the inheritor of a good part of his father's strength and courage. The divine arms of Achilles were naturally coveted by the surviving chieftains, and the leading claimants were Odysseus and the greater Aias. The Achaians adjudged them to the former, on the grounds that their Trojan prisoners declared that they feared him more than his rival. Aias went mad with disappointment and wounded pride, killed a number of sheep under the delusion that they were Achaian chiefs, and on coming to his senses commited suicide. As we have the story in Sophokles, Agamemnon ordered him to be left unburied, Teukros insisted that he be given on honourable funeral, and Odysseus, forgetting his rivalry, supported him and won Agamemnon over. The end was now approaching. Odysseus and Diomedes made their way into Troy and carried off the Palladion, an ancient and very holy image of Athena which was the 'luck' of the city. This is but one of several tales of how some magical obstacle to the taking of so strong a place was removed. Finally Epeios, a minor figure in the story hitherto, constructed an immense wooden horse, in which a picked body of men was concealed, while the rest of the army pretended to abandon the blockade and sail away. The Trojans were induced (for instance, in the version followed by Vergil, by an elaborate tale told them by one Sinon, who stayed behind and purposely let himself be made prisoner) to take it into the city, believing that it would bring them good fortune. In the night the hidden men came out, the rest returned from their temporary anchorage at the island of Tenedos, and the city was taken after sharp fighting in the streets. Priam was killed at the altar in his own courtyard by Neoptolemos. Paris had already fallen in battle; Deïphobos, who had succeeded him as husband to Helen, was killed by Menelaos; Aineias and several others escaped.

The women were divided among the conquerors, Andromache falling to the share of Neoptolemos, from whom, after he had been murdered at Delphoi by Orestes, she was passed to Helenos, who settled in Epeiros and founded a small city modelled on Troy there. Little Astyanax had been flung from the wall of Troy, since it was felt to be too dangerous to leave anyone of Hektor's stock alive. Old Hekabe was assigned to Odysseus, but did not return with him. Her one surviving son Polydoros had been sent out of Troy to the guardianship of Polymestor, a Thracian prince, who murdered him to get possession of the wealth he had brought with him. Warned by his ghost, Hekabe enticed Polymestor into her tent, where she and her women killed his children before his eyes and blinded him. She herself was finally transformed into a bitch, and died and was buried at a spot called in memory of her Kynos Sema ('the Bitch's grave'). Her daughter Polyxene was claimed as his share by the ghost of Achilles, and sacrificed at his tomb.

Of the surviving Greeks, Odysseus, Nestor and Menelaos sailed away independently. The story of the first will be told in the next chapter; Nestor arrived safely in Pylos, but Menelaos was carried by a storm to Egypt, and wandered for some time before returning to Greece, not unprofitably, however, for after the fashion of the day, he was hospitably entertained in various places and given guest-gifts before he left. However, when at last he was setting out from Egypt, he found himself weather-bound in what was then the island of Pharos, a little way from the then mouths of the Nile. He had the good fortune to excite the pity of a sea-nymph, who informed him that the surest way of escape was to capture her father Proteus, herdsman of the flocks of the sea, and so force him to impart some of his supernatural knowledge. She disguised Menelaos and three of his men in sealskins, and when Proteus came out of the water with his marine herd, he counted the men with the genuine sea-beasts, and lay down for a noonday siesta. Menelaos and his followers then seized and held him, although he took all manner of shapes, including water and fire. When at last he resumed his own form he was ready to comply with the request of Menelaos. The bad weather was due to his having neglected to make appropriate sacrifices before quitting Egypt; if he returned thither and made them, all would be well. Proteus then told him of the murder of Agamemnon, and assured him that he would reach home in time for the funeral feast of Aigisthos and Klytaimestra (p. 73). He himself was never to die, but be translated to the Elysian Plain (p. 59), because he was son-in-law to Zeus by virtue of his marriage to Helen. Of the rest, Odysseus was stayed on Kalypso's island (p. 144), and the lesser Aias had been drowned. He had torn Kassandra from the temple of Athena and violated her, thus incurring the wrath of the goddess, and was wrecked on the way home. Climbing out on to a rock, he boasted that he had got through safely despite the gods (this seems to be the origin of the modern allusion to 'Ajax defying the lightning', a thing neither hero of that name is ever said to have done), and Poseidon broke the rock and so threw him into the sea, where he perished.

This is the earliest (Homeric) account of the long tale of the Returns (*Nostoi*) of the fighters before Troy. Later writers greatly elaborated the story, and once more the figure of Palamedes appears. His father Nauplios was bent on revenge for his son, and after Athena had scattered the fleet with a storm, he burned false lights at Cape Kaphareus in Euboia, which sent many ships on to the rocks there. Sundry legends tell of the misfortunes which overtook those who escaped the storm and the false beacons, but their connexion with the Troy-saga proper is loose, and they are largely concerned with providing foundation-legends for various cities. Thus, Teukros is said to have been banished from Salamis by Telamon, because he returned without Aias; whereat he went to Cyprus and founded the city of Salamis there, naming it in memory of his old home. Diomedes found that his wife Aglaïe had been unfaithful to him, and his own life was in danger from treacherous assaults. He therefore left Argos, went to Italy, settled there, and finally was killed and his followers turned into sheerwaters, which henceforth showed their origin by behaving peaceably to Greeks, with hostility to others. Diomedes himself received a cult, i.e., by some process unknown to us a local deity came to be indentified with him.

V

MARCHEN

Attention has been drawn to the intrusion of folktales into many of the stories already told. In this chapter I discuss one famous work which on examination proves to be folktale using figures of saga for its characters, and a unique example of a folktale which is presented to us as such, with brief mention of some other remnants of ancient popular imagination comparable to that which has produced, among many other things, the numerous and interesting *märchen* (*paramythia* in modern Greek) which still survive.

The plot of Homer's *Odyssey* is connected with no Mycenaean site, for there is no evidence that any considerable centre of that culture existed on or even near Ithake. If, moreover, we look at the plot, we see that it is the widespread tale of how a man was so long absent from home that his wife gave him up as dead, and was on the point of marrying someone else when he returned and made himself known. The incidents also of his adventures are for the most part very unlike normal Greek saga, consisting as they do of encounters with monsters, witches and so forth in unknown lands; for I hold with some of the best opinion ancient and modern that it is vain to look for real places as the localities of the hero's wandering.

Odysseus, according to the poet, left Troy ill-satisfied with his share of the spoils, and to recoup himself and his men went on a piratical raid against a neighbouring people, the Kikones. After getting some plunder, however, he was heavily defeated by reinforcements from inland, and obliged to retreat in haste with his twelve ships. Storms then drove him to the land of the Lotos-Eaters, where some of his men tasted of the lotos (whatever exactly that wonderful plant may be), the virtue of which was to make them forget home and friends.

Forcing them to re-embark, he sailed on, but another storm drove him to an uninhabited island close to the country of the Kyklopes (p. 44). Next day he went with his own ship and crew across the intervening strait, and with twelve men entered the cave of one of the Kyklopes, who returning from pasturing his flocks caught them stealing his goods and shut them up in the cave, closing the entrance with a rock much too large for anyone not of his gigantic size and strength to move. He then proceeded to eat them two at a time for his breakfast and supper. Odysseus dared not kill him as he slept, for he would never be able to get out of the cave, but the second night he gave him some strong wine of which he had brought a skinful, and when he was thoroughly drunk, put out his one eye. Polyphemos, for that was the monster's name, roared till his fellows came to inquire what ailed him, to whom he replied that Nobody was killing him; Odysseus had told him that that was his name, and Polyphemos, not to be outdone in courtesy, had promised to eat him last of all. The others, supposing he must be ill, advised him to pray for relief to his father Poseidon, and so went away. In the morning he lifted the rock and Odysseus and his men managed to slip out unperceived among the sheep and get back to their ship. Even then they were in danger, for Odysseus taunted Polyphemos and in doing so mentioned his real name. Polyphemos, after missing the ship with two huge rocks, prayed to Poseidon that Odysseus, if he must return home, might arrive there alone and in evil plight, conveyed on a ship not his own, and find troubles awaiting him. Poseidon thenceforth was Odysseus' enemy, but Athena remained his staunch friend.

He next arrived at the island of Aiolos (not the Aiolos mentioned on p. 89), who by favour of the gods had possession of all the winds. After entertaining Odysseus and his men, he gave him as a parting gift a leather sack containing all the winds but the one which would take them home. When they were in sight of Ithake, Odysseus fell asleep and his men opened the sack, thinking it contained treasure. The winds rushed out and drove them back to Aiolos' island, from which they were repelled as being obviously out of favour with the gods. They then sailed away at random and arrived in the country of the Laistrygones, cannibal giants, who destroyed all the ships but Odysseus' own and ate their crews. Odysseus next reached the island of Aiaie, the home of Kirke the witch-goddess, a sister of Aietes (p. 122). On being visited by half Odysseus' crew, she offered them a magic drink which turned them into swine, save one who managed to escape and inform Odysseus. He then went alone to her house, but on the way encountered Hermes, who gave him the magic herb moly, the smell of which rendered him proof against enchantments. Baffled and threatened with Odysseus' sword, Kirke surrendered, swore not to harm him, restored his men to their proper form, and entertained them all for a year. Then, as he pressed her to tell him how to reach home, she bade him first go across the stream of Ocean to the world of the dead and inquire of the ghost of Teiresias (pp. 120 f.). This he did, using appropriate rites to enable the ghosts to speak to him, for which they needed a drink of the blood of black sheep. Teiresias informed him of matters at his home, foretold that he would overcome his rivals there, and added that he must afterwards go on a pilgrimage inland, carrying an oar, till he came to a place where the oar was mistaken for a winnowing-fan, and there establish a cult of Poseidon Returning, he should in the end find a quiet death 'from the sea'. Back in Aiaie, after holding converse with a number of other ghosts, he was given directions for his journey. He would first come to the land of the Seirenes (Sirens), who tempted sailors with their wonderful singing, and when they came near, wrecked and drowned them. Next he would sight the Planktai (Wandering rocks; the same as the Symplegades, cf. p. 126), which no ship except the Argo had ever passed. To avoid these he must sail through a strait which had on one side the terrible whirlpool Charybdis, on the other the six-headed monster Skylla (not the daughter of Nisos, p. 79), who caught and ate men. He must sail close to her, as being the less deadly, and get through to the island of Thrinakie, where the cattle of the Sun pastured. These he must by no means harm.

He duly set sail, and approaching the Seirenes, filled his men's ears with wax and had himself bound to the mast. The song was so enchanting, especially as it promised him all manner of knowledge, that he struggled to get loose, but his men bound him still tighter until they were out of hearing of the music. He then took the wax from their ears, avoided the

Planktai, and sailing through the strait, saw six of his men carried off by Skylla without being able to help them, although he stood armed and ready to resist. Coming to Thrinakie, they were stormbound and so short of food that they had to eat fish, the last resort of a starving man to the meat-eating Achaians. Without his knowledge, his men killed and cooked some of the cattle, and the Sun made complaint to Zeus, who promised to punish the committers of the sacrilege. The wind fell and Odysseus set forth again, but there came a violent storm accompanied by a thunderbolt which shattered the ship to pieces. Odysseus was the only survivor, and kept afloat by riding some of the wreckage, only to be carried towards Charybdis again. He therefore held on to a tree which grew above the whirlpool, until it began to cast its waters forth, as it did at intervals. Carried by the current, he escaped it, and after being afloat nine days and nights he came ashore on an island in the very middle of the sea, inhabited by a nymph, Kalypso ('the concealer'), who made him heartily welcome and wished to marry him, even promising him immortality if he would consent. He, however, wanted only to return home, and held out against her for seven years, during which time he was her lover, as he had been Kirke's. Meantime his wife, Penelope, was beset by suitors, the sons of the chief families of Ithake and the neighbouring islands, which also belonged to Odysseus' kingdom, or rather barony, and had no means of keeping them away. They lodged near Odysseus' palace and spent the day there, eating and drinking at the expense of the household stores and the flocks and herds belonging to him. For a while she put them off with the excuse that she must weave a shroud for old Laertes, Odysseus' father, who had long retired from the active duties of kingship in favour of his son, and could not be expected to survive for many years. She wove diligently every day, and every night unravelled her day's work; but one of her handmaids betrayed her and she was forced to complete the task. Meanwhile Telemachos, Odysseus' only son of Penelope, had come to young manhood, being about twenty years of age when the poem begins. Now Athena bestirred herself and, at a council of the gods in the absence of Poseidon, moved Zeus to order Kalypso to let Odysseus go. Meanwhile she went to Ithake in disguise and advised Telemachos to call a folkmoot and formally bid the suitors leave, and if they would not, to get a ship and go to the mainland in search of news of his father. He did so; the suitors scornfully rejected his proposal, but he, still with the help of Athena (who now took the shape of Mentor, an old friend of Odysseus), borrowed a ship and, with a volunteer crew of the young men of Ithake, visited first Nestor at Pylos, then Menelaos at Sparta.

Odysseus was now free to leave Kalypso, who, warned by Hermes of Zeus' order, gave him materials and tools to construct a makeshift ship. On this he sailed till he came in sight of land, and then was wrecked in a storm stirred up by Poseidon, who had caught sight of him on his way back from the Ethiopian festival he had been attending. Helped by Ino-Leukothea (p. 53), who gave him her wimple as a kind of magical life-belt, he finally got ashore and spent the night huddled in a hollow among dead leaves. In the morning Nausikaa, daughter of the king of the country, Alkinoos, came down to the river-mouth to wash the family linen. Odysseus woke at a noise her attendants made, approached her with courteous words, and got from her a suit of clothes, for he was naked, and much-needed food and drink, with directions how to approach the palace. There he got the favour of Alkinoos' queen Arete and of the king himself, was entertained and given handsome presents, and told the story of his adventures. He then was brought to Ithake in one of the ships of Alkinoos' subjects, the Phaiakians, who were wonderful sailors, possessed of vessels which knew their way everywhere and moved as fast as a bird can fly.

Now Athena intervened again. She bade Telemachos hasten home, returning by a different route, because the suitors were waiting for him on the course he had taken in going and meant to surprise and kill him. She met Odysseus, warned him that he must not visit his home openly, and disguised him as an old beggar. In this shape he was charitably received by one of his own thralls, Eumaios the chief swineherd, who longed for his return, and at his cottage met Telemachos and made himself known to him. He then went to the palace and begged of the suitors, commending himself to them by overcoming in fight a real beggar, Iros by name, whom he struck gently, so as not to reveal his true strength, merely breaking his jawbone. He took an opportunity to speak with Penelope, assuring her that her husband was alive and would soon return, and advising her to invite the suitors to a trial of skill. Whichever of them could string Odysseus' great bow and shoot an arrow from it through holes in the blades of a row of axes set up on end was to be her husband. Furthermore, he discovered that one other thrall, Philoitios the cattleman, was faithful to him, and that Eurykleia, Penelope's old nurse, could be depended upon, although she nearly betrayed him while washing his feet, for she recognized him by an old scar on his thigh. He and Telemachos removed all arms from the great hall on the eve of the contest, except four sets.

The suitors could hardly decline the test, and one by one they failed to string the bow. Finally, Odysseus asked, as if in jest, to be allowed to try, and was given the bow by Telemachos' order. He strung it easily, shot through the axes, and then shot down Antinoos, the leading suitor, revealed himself, and with the help of his three supporters killed all the rest. Now he took vengeance on the unfaithful, hanging those of the maids who had been the suitors' paramours and mutilating Melanthios the goatherd, who had sided with them and got them arms during the fight. Penelope was persuaded that it was indeed he, and not some god in disguise, by his mentioning to her a secret known only to themselves and Eurykleia, the peculiar construction of their bed. The next day he met and was recognized by his father, and he and his followers set out to meet the kinsmen of the suitors, who had by this time learned of the slaughter and were seeking revenge, as was indeed their duty by the customs of that day. Old Laertes, restored by miracle to his youthful vigour for the time being, killed the father of Antinoos, Zeus stopped the fighting with a thunderbolt, and Athena in the shape of Mentor arranged a peace. A later poet continued the story from where Homer left it off. Odysseus did as Teiresias had bidden and returned to Ithake. Now Telegonos, his son by Kirke, arrived on the island in search of his father. For some reason he began to ravage the country, and in the ensuing fight he met Odysseus, whom he did not recognize, and killed him with a spear pointed with fishbone, thus giving him in all literalness a 'death from the sea'.

The other folktale is one which has literally hundreds of

variants found in the most diverse regions of the world. It occurs as an episode in the famous *Metamorphoses* (otherwise *The Golden Ass*) of Apuleius (second century A.D.), and is written in his florid Latin, like the rest of the work, which is a fantastic romance, probably itself going back to some folktale, concerning one Lucius who by misusing magic was turned into an ass and after many adventures was able through the grace of Isis, whose votary he became, to recover his human shape by eating roses. The story is indeed an old wife's tale, for it is so described and is told by an old woman. In a certain city there were a king and queen who had three daughters, all handsome, but the youngest, Psyche (Butterfly?), of such extraordinary beauty that she was taken for Venus (=Aphrodite) herself and consequently her many admirers were afraid to propose marriage to her. On inquiring how to find her a husband, the king was bidden dress her as a bride and leave her on the top of a mountain. The reason for this was that the real Venus had sent Cupid (=Eros) to make Psyche fall in love with some ugly wretch, but instead of doing so he fell in love with her himself. Consequently, she was carried by a wind, his messenger, from the mountain-top to a marvellous palace, and there he visited her in the dark. After a while she longed for the company of her sisters, who on visiting her became extremely jealous of her good fortune, discovered that she had never seen her husband, and persuaded her that he was a cannibal monster. They provided her with a lantern and a knife, so that she might discover and kill him; but the lantern revealed his beauty as he lay asleep, and a drop of hot oil from it woke and hurt him. He flew away, Psyche grasping his leg until she dropped off from weariness. She then, after fruitless wanderings, went to Venus herself, who received her harshly and set her impossible tasks. The first was to sort out into separate heaps a mingled pile of different grains. This was done for her by a great swarm of ants, presumably Cupid's agents. Then she was sent to get water from the Styx, where it flows down a cliff-face in Arkadia. The stream was quite inaccessible, but an eagle snatched her pitcher, held it under the waterfall, and returned it full. Lastly she was sent to the underworld to get from Proserpina a box containing what was alleged to be beauty. Warned by a voice proceeding from a tower, from the top of which she had meant to throw herself and so be rid of her troubles once and for all, she avoided many snares besetting the road to the House of Hades, was given the mysterious casket, and on the way back had the curiosity to open it, hoping to make herself more attractive to her husband when they should meet again. But what it really contained was a deadly sleep which at once overpowered her. Now Cupid intervened in person. Being a god, he could deal with the sleep, which he rubbed off her and put back in the box, and while she was taking it to Venus, got Juppiter's consent to his marriage. Thus Psyche (the word can also mean 'soul', and it may be that an allegory underlies some part of the tale) became immortal.

No other folktale is recorded for us as such, but acquaintance with modern studies in *märchen*-themes enables us to recognize a few more, scattered up and down ancient literature. A few instances have been given (pp. 72, 77) of persons exposed and suckled by beasts. This is a stock theme, and there are scores of classical instances, some applied to historical persons. Animals of various kinds also appear in tales which again are sometimes connected with real historical figures. It is not surprising that some of them are poets, for, especially in early times, the line between a poet's verses and a magician's charms was not always very sharply drawn, and besides, poets were regularly said, and no doubt originally thought, to be directly inspired by the Muses. Hence such stories as the following. Arion, a lyric poet of the seventh century B.C., went on what we should describe as a concert tour of Italy and Sicily, and having got much wealth by his music, started back to Corinth, where he lived. His ship's crew plotted to throw him overboard and steal his wealth; he asked leave to sing once more before dying, and the sailors readily consented. Finishing his song, he leaped overboard and was taken on the back of a friendly dolphin, which brought him safe to Tainaron (Cape Matapan) in the Peloponnesos. His would-be murderers were duly detected and executed. Here we can guess with some plausibility how the tale arose. Herodotos says that there was at Tainaran a dedication of Arion's, a figurine of a man riding a dolphin. This group appears on coins of Taras (Tarentum), and it is likely enough that Arion bought it there and presented it to Poseidon's temple at Tainaron as a thank-offering for his safe return. The man is of course not Arion himself, but Taras, the eponym of the city. Another lyric poet was Ibykos, about a century later than Arion. He is said to have been murdered by certain ruffians, and to have called to a flock of cranes to do him justice. His killers later on saw some cranes fly overhead as they sat in a theatre, whereat one of them whispered to another, 'There go Ibykos' avengers'. He was overheard, and the crime detected. Yet another murderer was a certain Bessos, who had killed his own father. He was seen destroying a nest of young swallows, and on being asked for an explanation, declared that they were accusing him of patricide. This started an inquiry, and he too paid the penalty of his sin.

A famous theme (it occurs for instance in the Hebrew legend of Jephthah) is known as *Homecomer's Vow*. A man in difficulties swears to sacrifice the first thing that meets him on returning home safely, supposing that it will be some beast; alternatively, to give it to a devil or other supernatural or mysterious being who helps him. The former is the Greek version, as it is the Hebrew. Idomeneus, commander of the Cretan contingent before Troy, made this rash vow during a storm, and the first being to meet him on landing in Crete was his own son. He either sacrificed or tried to sacrifice him, and was exiled. Not unlike this are Agamemnon's vow (p. 130) and a story told of Alexander the Great. He was bidden by an oracle to sacrifice the first living thing that met him as he left a certain city. This proved to be an ass-driver, who however saved himself by pointing out that his ass had been actually the first to meet Alexander.

Many heroes of comparatively recent folklore outwit the devil in one way or another. There is no Greek devil, he being a native of quite another part of the world (Iran and large tracts of Asia and N. America), but Sisyphos of Corinth outwitted Death. When his time came to die, he left strict instructions that his body should be flung out with no funeral rites at all, a piece of gross impiety. Arriving before Hades, he begged leave to return to earth long enough to punish his wife Merope for her unnatural behaviour, and being allowed to do so, was very careful not to punish her, thus freeing himself from any obligation to die at all. This probably (cf. p. 59) is why, when at last his life did end, his punishment in the other world is everlasting; he had made himself immortal.

Murders are commonly enough exposed in European and other folklore by means of some part of the dead person, such as his hair or a bone, which is able to produce a sound (for instance, by being made into a musical instrument). Vergil seems to have learned of a tale of this kind and used it for an incident in the *Aeneid*. Aeneas, wanting wood, pulls some cornel-bushes and horrible sounds issue from beneath them; then a voice from the ground proclaims that that is the burial-place of his kinsman Polydoros (cf. p. 137), and the bushes have grown from the shafts of the spears with which he was killed.

Why men die and snakes (supposedly) do not, but change their skins and grow young again when they are old is a problem which has exercised the wits of many early thinkers. The Greek account is preserved by the learned Alexandrian poet Nikandros, who wrote among other works a versified account of snake-bites and how to cure them. Zeus sent mankind an ass-load of youth, but the ass grew thirsty and found the way to a nearby spring barred by a serpent, which demanded his load as the price of access to the water. The ass agreed, and so man never got the intended gift and serpents have it. Nikandros says, probably with truth, that it is a very old tale.

The peculiarities of birds and beasts furnish yet another very fruitful theme. We have had one instance in the story of Prokne and Philomela (p. 80). Homer alludes to another, and the ancient commentators on him tell us the whole tale. Aëdon (Nightingale) was wife of king Zethos (p. 86), and envied Niobe for her many children (p. 46); she plotted to kill them in the night, but instead mistook the bed in which her own son Itylos was sleeping and killed him. She mourned for him until the gods turned her into a nightingale, which still sings sadly. Yet another version exists, but is practically Prokne and Philomela again with the names changed. The halcyon, which so far as it is a real bird at all seems to be a sort of kingfisher, was alleged to nest on the sea at midwinter, the water remaining calm for some days till the eggs were hatched. Keyx, a son of the Morning Star (Phosphoros in Greek, Lucifer in Latin) had a wife Alkyone, to whom he was devoted and she to him. He was wrecked and drowned on a journey and his body came ashore at her feet; the gods pitied them both and turned them into the birds which bear her name. Another version is that the metamorphosis was a punishment for their impiety in calling themselves Zeus and Hera; *keyx* is one of several forms of the name of another bird, a kind of gull. These examples may suffice.

One famous tale has come down to us from Greece in two forms, one of them confessedly not native. Trophonios was a hero or a chthonian god (it is not always easy to differentiate), and had a famous oracle at Lebadeia in Boiotia, consultants at which had to go through a most remarkable and elaborate ritual before getting an answer. But the story concerning him and his brother Agamedes has nothing to do with these functions, except for the last incident in it, which looks suspiciously like an addition. The two were sons of king Erginos of Orchomenos, and became famous architects, building both temples and palaces. They made a treasury for Hyrieus the father of Orion (p. 47), but secretly arranged one of the stones so that it could be removed from without. When the treasures were put into the building, they used to come at night and help themselves. Hyrieus, puzzled by the disappearance of much of his wealth, set a trap, in which Agamedes was caught. Trophonios could not release him, and fearing that he would be found in the morning and tortured into revealing the whole secret, cut off his head. At this point (and here I suspect a pious addition to the legend) the earth yawned and swallowed Trophonios up; Agamedes was commemorated by a pit and a gravestone in his sanctuary. How the tale came to be connected with these divine or heroic figures and where it originated we cannot say; but it is interesting that Herodotos tells substantially the same story in an Egyptian setting. As he is scrupulous in recording what he was told, in foreign countries as in Greece, the probability is that he heard it from some Greek-speaking Egyptian. The owner of the treasury is here the Pharaoh 'Rampsinitos', presumably Ramses. The architect is not himself the thief, but leaves the secret to his two sons, who profit by it; the surviving thief escapes the king's attempts to catch him, and finally is reconciled to him and marries his daughter, on the grounds that while Egyptians excel all other men in cunning, he has excelled all other Egyptians.

VI

SOME LATER DEVELOPMENTS

The stories told hitherto, whether myths, sagas or *märchen*, are almost all entirely Greek in origin and were told by and for Greeks, who seem at least in the earlier periods to have believed the first two classes more or less literally. But after the career of Alexander the Great, in what is generally called the Hellenistic Age (from the last decades of the fourth century B.C. onwards), a revolutionary change took place. Greek culture spread over areas hitherto quite or almost unaffected by it, including great parts of the Near East, Egypt, and those parts of Italy which were not settled by Greeks, i.e., everything from the latitude of Naples north. Inevitably, the peoples who adopted this culture modified it, each contributing something of its own. Furthermore, as the traditional Greek religion weakened, because the gods worshipped by the various States had shown themselves unable to protect them from the conquering Macedonians, the myths concerning them were taken less and less seriously, at all events by the educated classes, for whom, rather than for the general public, the literature of this age was composed. For those who did not explain them according to one of the many theories in vogue, they became simply literary adornments, raw material for the learned kind of poetry most in favour, and were hardly more believed than they are by us. Sagas were treated as part of early history, admittedly not always exactly true, for poets of early date were credited, not without some justification, with having modified the facts and added their own inventions freely. Still, to have some connexion with these venerable legends was, one might say, a badge of respectability for any community small or large, and nothing was commoner than a literary account of the 'foundation' (*ktisis*) of such-and-such a city, or the origin (*aition*) of a traditional custom. Where, as in

the case of new foundations or foreign places hitherto unconnected with Greek tradition, no such legend existed, or none
was known to writers and speakers of Greek, it was not unusual to invent one, as we shall see in the case especially of
Rome.

Using mythology as an ornament, writers and especially
poets of the new age naturally looked about for new tales,
which had not already been sufficiently handled by the great
writers of the past, for whom they had generally a vast
reverence, the more so as most authors were themselves also
scholars, busy in cataloguing, commenting upon or criticizing
the text-tradition of the classics from Homer down. This is
why not a few of the stories already told have come down to
us either in the surviving works of the Alexandrians, as
literary men of that age are often called, from the circumstance that Alexandria in Egypt was one of the principal
centres of scholarly activity and of original work, or from
authors, generally Latin, who drew upon them. Another
common resource was to rehandle traditional tales so as to
emphasize the romantic side (practically all the great love-
stories either are actually Alexandrian or have Alexandrian
parallels and prototypes), to adorn them with rhetorical
speeches and descriptions, and to humanize the superhuman
characters in them till no trace, or very little, of their divinity
is left. Thus the most famous of Alexandrian poets, Kallimachos, wrote hymns to various gods, which survive. In one
of them he describes the childhood of Artemis, and she
appears simply as a bold and attractive little girl, coaxing
Zeus to give her what she wants and playing unafraid with
the Kyklopes of Hephaistos' forge. Apollonios of Rhodes
shows us Hera and Athena approaching Aphrodite to induce
her to make Medeia love Jason. It is a good portrayal of two
great ladies constrained to ask a favour of one who is neither
socially nor morally their equal; and it leads up to a description of Medeia's emotions comparable to the psychological
subtleties of good modern novels rather than the broad
pictures of the older epic. Obviously, this could, and too often
did, degenerate into sentimentality and trifling, and indeed
we repeatedly meet the complaint, in the later literature
especially, that the traditional themes are hackneyed and no
longer interesting, and find many attempts to discover some-

thing fresh to write about. With various experiments, such as didactic poetry, which took other than mythological subjects we are not now concerned; but one novelty calls for attention. It was a time when astromony was making great strides, and at the same time astrology was rapidly gaining ground in both learned and popular belief and a philosophic astral religion was widely spread. Hence it is not remarkable that astral myths were very much in favour. We have seen (p. 47) that these were very rare among the older authors, and so presumably in the older beliefs and fancies; but now we come across one tale after another which is brought into relation to the stars, especially to those human or animal figures which a lively pictorial imagination saw in the constellations, giving them the names by which they are still known. There is, for instance, a little treatise falsely ascribed to Eratosthenes (flourished about 275-194 B.C.), poet, geographer, scholar, mathematician and astronomer, from which we learn the following additions to tales already told. Ursa Maior was once Kallisto (p. 48). Ursa Minor was a nymph seduced by Zeus. Draco was the dragon which guarded the apples of the Hesperides (p. 110), and the kneeling figure (*Engonasin*), as the ancients called it, is Herakles fighting the dragon, hence its common modern name Hercules. The Northern Crown is the wedding-garland which Dionysos gave Ariadne (p. 82). Ophiuchus is Asklepios with the snakes which he, like many chthonian gods and heroes, has as his attendants. Zeus placed him among the stars to console Apollo for his death (cf. p. 43). The Scorpion is the one which stung Orion to death (p. 48); Bootes or Arctophylax (cf. 49) Kallisto's son, still attendant on his mother. Virgo is either Justice or one of the greater goddesses, Greek or foreign. The Twins are Kastor and Polydeukes (p. 74). Cancer is the crab which helped the hydra (p. 106) against Herakles. Certain stars in it are known as the Asses, and they were ridden by Hephaistos and the Satyrs when they went out to do battle with the Giants. Their braying frightened the enemy, and for that good service they were rewarded in this manner. Leo is the Nemean lion (p. 106). Auriga is Erichthonios (p. 37), the first of mankind to yoke horses to a chariot; Zeus admired him for imitating the chariot of the Sun, and so made a constellation of him. Some, however, say he was Myrtilos, Oinomaos' charioteer (p. 72). Taurus is the

bull which brought Europê to Crete; in this version he is a
real bull, not Zeus disguised (p. 94). A whole group of constellations belongs to the story of Perseus; they include the
hero himself, Andromeda, her father Kepheus and her
mother Kassiepeia (cf. p. 103). The Horse is Pegasos (p. 34).
Aries is the ram which carried Phrixos and Helle (p. 122),
made immortal by Nephele. The Pleiades, which are a cluster
of seven stars, one nearly invisible to the naked eye, in the
forehead of the Bull, are daughters of Atlas (p. 67), Elektra,
mother by Zeus of Dardanos, founder of the Trojan dynasty,
Maia (p. 26), Taygete, on whom Zeus begat Lakedaimon,
the eponym of the district in which Sparta lies, Alkyone,
Kelaino, Sterope and Merope, of whom the last, unlike her
sisters, had no better than a mortal consort, Sisyphos (p. 149),
and so hides herself for shame. The Lyre is the one Hermes
made on his first day (p. 51), which afterwards was given by
Apollo to Orpheus (p. 90). Cycnus is the swan whose shape
Zeus took when he wooed Nemesis (p. 74), who laid in
consequence the egg from which Helen was hatched. Aquarius
is Ganymedes, son of Laomedon of Troy (p. 112), whom the
gods, or Zeus, carried off to be their cupbearer, because of his
beauty. This involves assuming that the liquid he pours from
his urn is nectar, not water. Capricorn is a son of Pan, who
was brought up in Crete with the young Zeus and later
invented the shell-trumpet, the noise of which struck 'panic'
fear into the Titans. Sagittarius is either a Centaur, or else a
certain Krotos (Applause), who won the favour of the
Muses. Sagitta is the arrow with which Apollo killed the
Kyklopes (p. 44). Aquila is the eagle which carried off
Ganymedes. The Dolphin earned his promotion to a constellation by his service to Poseidon. Amphitrite (p. 34) did not
want to marry him, and hid, but the dolphin found her and
brought her to him. Of Orion something has already been
said (p. 47). Canis is the always successful hound (p. 61); in
this version of the story the fox was turned to stone, the
hound made a constellation. The Argo commemorates the
famous voyage (p. 123). Cetus is the sea-monster which was
about to devour Andromeda. The Milky Way is Hera's
breast-milk. No son of Zeus might gain heaven unless Hera
suckled him, consequently Hermes brought the infant
Herakles to her; but recognizing the child as none of hers, she

shook him off and the milk spirted out and formed the Galaxy.

Mythology was in this state when the Romans became acquainted with it, from the third century B.C. on. They seem to have had no myths of their own. To them, gods and goddesses were beings whose one important characteristic, so far as mankind was concerned, was the possession of that supernatural power which, at least from the second century B.C. onwards, was called in Latin *numen*. Properly approached, they could be induced and helped to exercise this on behalf of their worshippers, Ceres and Tellus for instance making the earth yield its fruits, Mars warding off various evils and so forth. What they were like personally, whether they had sex (grammatical gender their names had of necessity), and the hundred and one other details with which the Greeks concerned themselves were questions which seem never to have excited the more sluggish Roman imagination. But their admiration of Greek learning and ingenuity was as great as their contempt for most of the Greeks whom they met, especially as fighters, and they gladly received the foreign myths with or without the various philosophical criticisms of them. It seems to have been tacitly assumed by ancient nations that they all worshipped the same gods under different names, somewhat as they all used much the same domestic animals, etc., though they had different words for them. So Greek and Roman deities were identified wholesale. Kronos was taken as being the same as Saturnus, a deity of uncertain origin and functions, whose festival (cf. p. 30) resembled the Kronia. Zeus was rightly equated with Juppiter, Hera with Juno, who though not originally associated with Juppiter in cult had functions resembling Hera's in many ways. Ares was equated with Mars, who was really a much greater god and of far wider activities. Apollo was simply taken over, name and all, for no Roman or other Italian deity resembled him. Artemis was thought to be the same as Diana, resemblance in some functions being again the reason. Aphrodite was Latinized into Venus, who seems to have been in reality a rather insignificant little deity worshipped by market-gardeners to begin with; how she rose to be a great goddess is an obscure problem never fully solved as yet. The bond between them was possibly that Venus' functions somewhat resembled those of the Charites (p. 25), who commonly attend on Aphrodite. Athena was identified with Minerva, patroness of craftsmen and, as Rome grew less rustic and more literate, also of writers and scholars. Hermes was identified with Mercurius, if indeed Mercurius, god of tradesmen, was not originally Hermes himself given a Latin title (*merces*=merchandise). Herakles had long ago been received into the very heart of the City, his altar standing in the cattle market (Forum Boarium), near the oldest settlement on the Palatine, thus giving that place of trade with foreigners who came to buy hides or other products of the herds the necessary divine protection. Italian mouths mispronounced his name as Hercules. A sort of parallel to Poseidon was found in Neptunus, a not very important deity of fresh waters. Hephaistos was not unintelligently identified with Volkanus (Vulcan), who, like him, seems to have begun as a god of volcanic fires. Demeter found her counterpart in the corn-goddess Ceres, while Kore-Persephone was taken over in two different ways. Her name was distorted into Proserpina, and an absurd Latin etymology found for it; but also she and Dionysos were identified with an old divine pair, Liber and Libera, god and goddess of viticulture and the making of wine. Also, since Dionysos had long been identified with an Eleusinian godling, Iakchos, a triad was introduced into Roman worship at an early date, Ceres, Liber and Libera, that is the Eleusinian deities, Demeter, Iakchos and Kore. Pluton was sometimes merely latinized into Pluto, sometimes translated as Dis, the shorter form of *diues* ('rich'). Pan, who really had some resemblance to Faunus, a kind of fairy or goblin haunting uncultivated places, naturally was identified with him, and Faunus' epithet Siluanus (belonging to the *siluae*, the districts, especially wooded ones, which lay beyond the farmlands) was pressed into service as an equivalent for Seilenos, the Satyrs becoming on occasion Fauni, when not simply called by their Greek name. Juno had a title Lucina, 'she of the light', in her capacity as a goddess of birth, who brings children into the light of day; this provided an equivalent for Eileithyia, and Hebe was Latinized as Iuuentas. Hestia and Vesta were regarded as the same person, functionally with justice, though their etymological identity is a disputed point. A few deities for whom no Greek equivalent could be found were left unexplained, for instance Janus the two-faced god of gates and entrances of all kinds, and so of beginnings generally, or given wildly wrong identifications, for example the very obscure goddess Furrina, who was now and then equated with the Furiae, the Latin translation of Erinyes (via the cognate verb *erinyein*, 'to rage like an Erinys', which means much the same as Lat. *furere*, 'to be raving mad').

Hence it is that when a Latin, generally a poet, says that Juppiter overthrew Saturn, he means that Zeus defeated Kronos; if he refers to the loves of Mars and Venus, he means Ares and Aphrodite, and so forth. It is quite rare and generally only in passing, as an episode in a longer story, that a Latin ventures to frame a myth of his own concerning any deity, and then it is regularly on a Greek model. Exceptions are a few stories of the miracles of Roman gods and goddesses, if even those are not inspired by the similar tales (*aretai* as the Greeks called them) current at Greek shrines. For instance, it was said that a Vestal virgin, by name Aemilia, was accused of impiety, the evidence being that the goddess's holy fire, which burned perpetually, had gone out. She prayed that her innocence might be made manifest, and tearing a piece off her robe, threw it on the cold ashes. It straightway blazed up. Unchastity was the alleged offence of Tuccia, and a Vestal guilty of that was shut up alive in an underground cell in the Field of Ill-luck (Campus Sceleratus), there to starve or smother. She carried water from the Tiber in a sieve, by the power of the goddess, and was triumphantly cleared. A slandered matron, Claudia Quinta, was vindicated, not by Vesta, but by the Mother of the Gods, when her holy black stone was brought from Pessinus to Rome in 204 B.C. The ship conveying it up the Tiber mysteriously stuck fast; Claudia appealed to the Great Mother, grasped the tow rope, and single-handed pulled the vessel along. But of genuine Latin stories at all comparable to the many Greek tales of the dealings of the gods with one another, or with men of ancient days, and especially of their marriages, intrigues and offspring, there is not one demonstrable instance.

Sagas are perhaps not entirely wanting; at least a few stories, as much *märchen* as saga, need not have a Greek or other foreign source. There is one tale in particular, told of two notable people, Caeculus founder of the town of Praeneste and

Servius Tullius last but one of the seven traditional kings of
Rome, which may be genuinely native. Stripped of various
fanciful additions, it is to this effect. A girl of marriageable
age spent a night near a hearth-fire, generally in consequence
of some portent displayed in the flames. She became pregnant
and her son was in the one case Servius, in the other Caeculus.
We have here a very widespread theme, dependent upon the
common popular identification of life, light and heat (because
a living person is warm, a corpse cold). The fire put life into
her, quite literally.

But the process of manufacturing foundation-legends went
on, beginning early and continuing fairly late. To be really
respectable, a city must have a Greek origin, or failing that a
Trojan one; and conversely, if a city was admittedly important and powerful, it must go back to such a beginning.
Rome at various dates claimed both. The earliest settlement of
all, in prehistoric times, was Arkadian, led by king Euander
(probably 'strong-man', appropriate since the name Roma
sounds like a fairly common Greek word for strength). In his
day Hercules came there with the cattle of Geryon, some of
which were stolen from him by a formidable brigand, Cacus,
son of Vulcan (the evidence is fairly clear that he and his sister
Caca are a very ancient pair of fire-deities worshipped
presumably in the Palatine settlement, where the staircase of
Cacus, the *scala Caci*, is yet to be seen), and hidden away in a
cave. Hercules heard them low as he was driving the rest
away, broke into the cavern and killed Cacus, despite his fiery
breath. In gratitude, Euander and his people instituted a cult
of the hero at the Most High Altar (Ara Maxima) in the
Forum Boarium. The reason why these legendary settlers were
represented as Arkadians is probably the identification of the
very old rite of the Lupercalia with the Arkadian festival
of Lykaia (Lat. *lupus*= Gk. *lykos*=wolf), helped out by the
supposed identity of Pan and Faunus and the allegation that
the Lupercalia were held in honour of the latter. However, the
main account, made immortal especially by Vergil in the
Aeneid, begins with Aeneas and his adventures after the fall of
Troy (p. 137). Escaping from the burning city, he took with
him his father and his little son Iulus or Ascanius, destined to
be the ancestor of the *gens Iulia* to which among other famous
men Julius Caesar belonged, but lost his wife Creusa. A

considerable number of Trojans also escaped and managed to rescue a certain amount of treasure. After the Greeks departed, they built ships and set forth in search of a promised land in the west (Hesperia). After some six year's wandering, they came to Sicily, where Aeneas' kinsman Acestes had settled. There old Anchises died. Leaving Acestes, Aeneas was caught in a violent storm sent by Juno and driven towards Africa, finally arriving at Carthage, which had just been founded by the Tyrian princess Dido. Juno plotted to keep him there, and at her instigation Venus contrived that Dido should fall violently in love with him; but Juppiter sent Mercury to remind him of his obligation to reach Hesperia (Italy, as by this time he knew), and he accordingly set forth. Dido killed herself, first formally cursing him and all his people, and imprecating eternal war between her successors and his. He now returned to Sicily, celebrated funeral games in honour of the anniversary of his father's death, and after losing some ships which the women set on fire at Juno's instigation, left behind the weakest of his following and at last reached the mouth of the Tiber. At first his relations with the inhabitants and their king Latinus were friendly, but a quarrel, fanned to flame by Juno, soon broke out. Latinus and Aeneas agreed to seal their alliance by the marriage of the former's daughter Lavinia to the Trojan, for her destiny was to marry a foreigner. But she had another suitor, Turnus prince of the Rutulians, who defended his right by pointing out that he was ultimately of non-Italian origin. A trifling incident led to armed conflict, and both sides sought allies, Aeneas appealing to Euander and getting through him the command of an Etruscan army in rebellion against their tyrannous king Mezentius, but hampered by a prophecy to the effect that they must have a foreigner to lead them. Turnus was reinforced by Mezentius himself with such followers as he had, and contingents from many peoples of Italy. After a series of battles, mostly in favour of the Trojans and their allies, it was agreed to settle the matter by a single combat betwen Aeneas and Turnus. This was interrupted by a treacherous attack on Aeneas, which led to a general engagement, but afterwards the duel was fought and Turnus killed. Here the *Aeneid* ends; the story is diversified by episodes of true epic type, Aeneas' account of his earlier adventures to Dido, long descriptions of the games over Anchises and the mustering of the Italians to aid Turnus, and, most impressive of all, a visit to the lower world, in which Aeneas meets the beatified spirit of his father and is shown something of the future destiny of Rome. He is vouchsafed another glimpse of what is to come when Venus persuades Vulcan to make him divine arms, for the shield is decorated with scenes from Roman history, culminating in the victory of Augustus at the Battle of Actium. The historians and lesser poets give us the sequel. Ascanius founded Alba Longa and quitted his father's little kingdom of Lavinium, from which Aeneas had mysteriously disappeared in a battle and henceforth was worshipped as Iuppiter Indiges. He became the father of a long line of kings. One of these, Numitor, was dethroned by his ambitious brother Amulius, who, as Numitor had no sons, took measures to prevent his daughter Rea Silvia from having offspring by making her a Vestal. Mars, however, loved her and she bore twins, Romulus and Remus. The former name is one of the most unconvincing inventions in all the foundation-legends, Greek or other, for it is a by-form of *Romanus* and means simply 'Roman'. Both children were put into something which would float and set adrift in the flooded Tiber. They came ashore at the spot where a sacred fig-tree, the Ficus Ruminalis, grew, and there were suckled by a she-wolf (the wolf is Mars' beast), and found by a shepherd called Faustulus (probably a by-form of Faunus), who brought them home to his wife Acca Larentia (the name of a minor Roman goddess). The twins grew to young manhood and proved enterprising and valiant. One day Remus was captured and accused, truly or falsely, of brigandage; Romulus set out to rescue him, having first been told the secret of his origin so far as Faustulus knew it. He and Numitor, before whom Remus was being tried, were made known to each other; by a bold stroke the twins killed Amulius, restored Numitor and freed their mother from imprisonment. They then set out to build a city at the place where they had been found. They easily collected men to be the future citizens; an augury from the flight of vultures pointed out Romulus as king; Remus, who in jest leaped over the walls which his brother had begun to make, was killed by him or one of his followers for his sacrilege (a city wall, save for its gates, was a holy and inviolable thing). Thus Romulus had sole power, and after a reign of forty years he mysteriously disappeared during a thunderstorm. A little later his glorified form appeared to a citizen called Julius Proculus and announced that he was now a god and to be worshipped under the name of Quirinus. His wife Hersilia was joined to him in cult with the new title of Hora Quirini.

We need not linger over the reigns of the other six kings, they vary in historicity from Numa Pompilius, the second king, to Tarquinius Superbus, the last. Numa at least has a good Italian name, but the facts about him, if he ever existed, have quite disappeared under a welter of manifestly late and artificial tales. Generally speaking, any ancient law or custom which was not supposed to go back to the very beginnings of the City was credited to him. Tarquinius was the third of an Etruscan dynasty, which was certainly real, as archaeological and other evidence show, but the accounts of him have been so coloured by Greek stories of the rise and fall of tyrants that they are of little worth either for a historian or for a mythologist.

The kings, however, provided material for a number of aetiological stories, largely Greek in inspiration and some no doubt actually of Greek origin. For instance, it was said, and linguistic and other facts support the tradition, that the Roman people was of mixed origin, partly Latin and partly Sabine. Also, in their marriage customs as in those of many peoples, the separation of the bride from her father's household was indicated by a pretence of violence; she was formally pulled away from the embrace of her mother. A minor detail was that during the conveying of the bride to her future husband's house it was customary to shout *talassio,* a word the meaning of which was and still is unknown. All these things were accounted for by a single ingenious tale. Romulus' followers were all men, and he could get no wives for them from neighbouring cities. He therefore invited the Sabines to a festival, and during it he and his men carried off the visitors' unmarried women. The Sabines, under their king Titus Tatius, at once declared war, and fighting went on for some time till the women, now quite reconciled to their enforced marriages, ran between the contending armies and prevailed on both sides to make peace. A combined Roman-Sabine community resulted, Titus Tatius ruling with Romulus until he was assassinated in consequence of a quarrel with the people of Lavinium. During the kidnapping of the women, one was secured by the retainers of a man called Talassius, and to prevent interference, they cried out that they were taking her 'for Talassius' (*Talassio*). The marriage was a happy one, and thus the ritual cry originated.

This was not the only way in which the war with the Sabines was used to explain old and obscure matters. There was a cult on the Capitoline Hill of an ancient but minor deity called Tarpeia, obviously somehow connected with the Tarpeian Rock, the most precipitous part of the hill. Something about it would seem to have suggested funeral ritual, and this was explained as follows, clearly by someone who did not realize that hero-cult, or the worship of individual ghosts thought to be powerful, is not Roman. Tarpeius, commander of the garrison of the Capitol, had a daughter Tarpeia, who fell in love with Titus Tatius, or was tempted by him in some way to betray the stronghold. It was agreed that she should have what his soldiers wore on their left arms; she meant their gold bracelets, but once the place was taken she was instead crushed under the weight of their shields. There was another cult, of Juppiter Stator. The received explanation was that during a fierce fight in the Forum, Romulus prayed to the god to make his men stand fast (*stare*), and his prayer was answered.

As Tarpeia in the legend just mentioned becomes a woman and not a goddess, so with several other mythical figures. One reason for this is certainly the theory known as Euhemerism, from its originator, Euhemeros of Messene. He embodied in a romance the hypothesis that the conventional gods were really noteworthy persons, kings and queens for the most part, who had been given divine honours out of gratitude or flattery. This theory, which does not seem to have made much impression on the Greeks, became quite popular in Rome, especially after Ennius (239-169 B.C.) had made it known in a Latin treatise. Hence it is that we find Saturn (i.e., Kronos) and Janus converted into early kings; the latter received the former kindly when he took refuge in Italy, and he founded a town, Saturnia, on the site of the future Rome. Both kings were great civilizers, who taught their people useful arts, Janus navigation and Saturn agriculture. The true

Age of Gold was, according to one account, in Italy while
Saturn was king there, Janus, deified after his death, showed
his power when the Sabines took advantage of Tarpeia's
treachery, for he made hot springs gush out and scald them
as they assailed the Capitol, which is why the double arch
which embodied him was always left open in time of war, so
that nothing should prevent him from coming to the help
of his people whenever they needed it.

Quite a complicated story grew up around another ancient
figure of cult, Acca Larentia, whom we have already met
(p. 162) humanized into the wife of the humanized Faustulus.
She too becomes a woman in this tale, and one of none too
good reputation. In the simplest version it was she who
suckled the Twins, not a literal she-wolf, for *lupa* can mean
both 'she-wolf' and 'prostitute', and her morals were of the
loosest. The more elaborate tale makes her a professional
prostitute. The keeper of the temple of Hercules, having
nothing to do, played dice, one throw for himself and one for
Hercules. This was rash, for Hercules was not merely, as in
Greece, a potent averter of evil (*alexikakos*), but a positive
bringer of good luck, who could for instance guide a man to
where treasure was hidden. The god therefore naturally won.
The stake was a good dinner and the company of a pretty
wanton, so Acca Larentia was sent for to pass the night in the
temple. The god made himself known to her, and advised
her, when she left in the morning, to make friends with the
first man she met. This was a wealthy bachelor, who when he
died made her his heir; she in turn left her fortune to the
Roman people at her death, and was honoured accordingly.

These are not the only Euhemerized figures of cult who
appear in such artificial legends. Perhaps the quaintest example
is the treatment of the woodpecker (*picus*), who is Mars' sacred
bird. Of him we have a thoroughly Alexandrian story of
shape-changing and love-affairs. He was once a king, Picus
by name, who was very handsome and much sought after, but
his one love was the nymph Canens (Singer), daughter of
Janus by the nymph, or rather goddess, Venilia. Kirke, prowl-
ing in the woods to gather magic herbs, saw him and was at
once enamoured; her residence had long ago been fixed by
Greek settlers at the promontory called Circeii after her.
Attracting him towards her by a phantom wild boar which

he pursued, she told him of her love, but he rejected her, and in rage she turned him into the bird which thereafter bore his name.

Many legends, however, are rather better than these fancies, and may now and then preserve some fragment of real native tradition. A number group themselves around the story of Aeneas, which had already been forming for several generations before Vergil took it for his subject. As every house had its Vesta, the hearth, and its Di Penates, the gods of the storeroom (*penus*), so the state had its Vesta publica and its Penates publici, in origin respectively the hearth and the guardians of the storeroom of the king's house. The Penates for some reason were profoundly reverenced. We need not go into the complicated and learned theories which were constructed around them; it is enough to remember that they were generally considered to be Trojan deities brought with him by Aeneas. But they had their own miracle on record. Originally their images or emblems were at Lavinium, where Aeneas put them. In reverence, it was sought to transfer them to Alba Longa or Rome, but they would have none of it, and vanishing from their new residence returned of themselves to the old one.

A scattering of legends concerning ancient worthies from Aeneas down seem to contain fragments of real native tradition mixed with much that is foreign, at least in the versions which have survived to us. Aeneas was bidden to look for a place where he should find a white sow with thirty farrow; he found them at the site of Lavinium, and ages later Varro, the greatest of Roman scholars (116-27 B.C.), was shown their pickled bodies there, whether preserved as the result of some genuine local tale or manufactured to accord with what was by that time an accepted piece of early history we cannot say. Also, Aeneas was told that he never would settle until hunger drove him and his followers to eat their tables as well as the food on them. This prophecy too was fulfilled, for he and his men, on landing, used flat cakes of bread to put the rest of their food on, and finished by eating the bread. Stories of how events were foretold and came to pass in unexpected ways are so common that it is in no way impossible that they existed in early Italy. Aeneas need not of course have been the original hero of this one.

166

Plays on words also have probably interested men since articulate speech began, and therefore it is not necessary to suppose the core of the following tale to be an importation or a learned invention; one at least of the puns is Latin and not Greek. There was a strange old rite for the expiation (*procuratio*) of thunderbolts, that is to say of anything struck by lightning, for that, until the discovery of its electrical nature, was regularly supposed to be the descent of some kind of heavy and pointed missile from the skies. However explained, it was a portent, and measures must be taken to put all right with the deity concerned, in this case Juppiter. Good king Numa caught Faunus and Picus by mixing wine with a spring from which they commonly drank and so intoxicating them, and they explained to him how to summon Juppiter. On being questioned, the god demanded the sacrifice of a head (*caput*; it can imply a life among other things). Numa promptly added 'of garlic', and Juppiter then added 'human', to which the king supplied 'hair'. Still unappeased, Juppiter specified 'a life' and Numa added 'of a sprat'. The god laughed and agreed, and the materials for the rite were thenceforth garlic, some human hairs and a small fish. Whoever invented the story, the boldness of Numa and the readiness with which Juppiter allows himself to be led into verbal traps savour strongly of popular imagination.

It was in Numa's time also that a shield of archaic form fell from heaven. It was a sort of mascot or luck-piece, and Numa took precautions against it being stolen, by having eleven more made exactly like it. The artificer was a certain Mamurius, and his name was ever afterwards mentioned in the extremely ancient and unintelligible hymn which the priestly college of the Salii (Dancers) sang as they made their rhythmical movements with the shields and the rest of their old-fashioned equipment, in honour of Mars and Quirinus, on certain days of the year. Here Mamurius seems to have arisen, activity as an artisan and all, from a phrase of the hymn, *mamuri ueturi,* whatever it may have meant, coupled no doubt with a desire to know why the *ancilia,* as they were called, were holy.

Tullus Hostilius, the third king, also attempted to evoke Juppiter, whose title of Elicius refers to the possibility of causing him to appear. But he was less skilled or less pious or

both than Numa, and the only result was a thunderbolt which
destroyed him and his house.

The portentous birth of Servius Tullius has already been
mentioned (p. 161); except for it, there is little more in the
legends of the seven kings which needs to be recorded. A good
deal of what is said of them is suspected, not without reason,
of being the construction of Roman lawyers, interested in
such things as the limitations of magisterial power (*imperium*)
and the origins and exact significance of juridical and other
procedure. This is not mythology.

The Republic was ill-supplied with legends of any sort, or
at all events very few have come down to us, unless we count
the obviously romantic and unhistorical handling of sundry
real events by patriotic annalists. Two or three seem worth
mentioning. There was a praetor, that is to say a holder of the
magistracy next in seniority to the consuls, who was going
forth to war when suddenly horns (a well-known emblem of
power) grew upon his head. He naturally consulted an expert,
and was told that when he returned he would become king of
Rome; but being much too good a republican to want any
such thing, he never returned and went instead into voluntary
exile. In memory of his virtuous act, a bronze head with horns
on it was set up over the gate by which he left the city. The
head no doubt was real enough; it is a type known from
Etruscan art, the influence of which on early Rome was very
considerable. The story would sooner or later grow up from
it. The patriot's name is given as Genucius Cipus, why we
do not know.

A spot in the Forum was known as the Lacus Curtius, the
Curtain lake or cistern. As the ground had formerly been
undrained and swampy, this is not surprising in itself, but
curiosity arose as to who the Curtius in question was. One
explanation was that he was a Sabine leader, Mettius Curtius,
who was bogged there during the fighting in the Forum in the
days of Romulus (p. 163), another that he was a consul in
whose time the spot was struck by lightning and, according
to the usual custom, fenced in as being too holy or uncanny
to be trodden upon. But the best known and finest story is
that the ground once mysteriously opened at that point and
the diviners informed the Romans that it would never close
until they threw in their most valuable possession. There was a

young and valiant man, Marcus Curtius by name, who realized
that they had nothing more precious than such men as he was.
He therefore rode his horse into the chasm, which closed
above him, and it was named from him.

Another Republican tale is a manifest borrowing from
Greek (cf. p. 75). Not long after the expulsion of Tarquin,
the famous Battle of Lake Regillus was allegedly fought
between the Romans and the cities of the Latin League, and
resulted in a decisive victory for the former. According to
the more sober account preserved in Livy, the Roman
victory was due largely to the efforts of their cavalry-men,
who reinforced the infantry by fighting on foot at a critical
moment; and in accordance with this, the Roman commander,
the dictator Aulus Postumius, vowed a temple to Castor
(p. 74), who in Roman cult so overshadows his brother
that the pair are often called the Castores. But the Greek
historian Dionysos of Halikarnassos paints a much more
detailed picture of the battle (it need hardly be said that
both accounts of the fighting are as fictitious as anything else
in the story) and reports that two young horsemen of more
than human size were seen leading the Roman cavalry to
attack the Latins. Furthermore, according to him, two mysterious messengers appeared in Rome that evening leading
sweating horses, reported the victory, and then, after washing
their horses at the well in the Forum near Vesta's shrine, rode
away and were not to be found. This is not the only occasion on which the brothers (whose temple in the Forum still
partly stands, an impressive and famous ruin) showed their
favour to Rome. The third Macedonian War had dragged
out to a greater length than the relative strength of the two
parties warranted, thanks largely to the incompetence of the
Roman commanders. When finally the able Lucius Aemilius
Paulus won a decisive victory over Perses, the last king of
Macedonia, in 168 B.C., word of it was brought by two young
men on white horses to a certain Publius Vatinius, who when
he reported the news to the Senate was imprisoned for his
pains until official confirmation was received, after which he
was set free and handsome amends made to him. It is possible
that this is not pure legend. We know nothing of the psych-
ology of this obscure Vatinius, and it is quite conceivable that
in the general anxiety and excitement which seems to have

prevailed he had a genuine hallucination. But the influence of the story of the Sagra (p. 75) is patent, and the resemblance is noticed by Cicero, to whom we owe our best account of the vision.

I omit sundry stories of Roman or other Italian deities, to be found especially in Ovid, with nothing to indicate that they were not simply invented by him. But there is one so famous and yet so patently artificial that it is worth mentioning; our main authorities for it are Vergil and his ancient commentators. At the grove (*nemus*) of Diana from which the modern village of Nemi takes its name, there was a cult of a god called Virbius, of whom we know practically nothing and the ancients apparently not much more. Some ingenious person found an etymology for his name, *uir bis,* 'a man twice', and set about explaining this. There was a version of the story of Hippolytos (p. 83) according to which he was brought to life again by Asklepios (cf. p. 44), no doubt at the request of Artemis, who had long been identified with Diana. Here then was a mythological explanation of the mysterious figure; Virbius had been a man, died, and being brought to life was a man once more, and immortal to boot. If confirmation of the theory was needed, a tabu observed at the grove furnished it; Hippolytos' horses had dragged him to death, and horses were not allowed in the sacred place.

Since mythology was to become no more than a literary ornament, receiving at best the amount of quasi-belief which it may on occasion with us, the traditional stories might be altered and added to for the most frivolous purposes by anyone. To know them was part of everyone's literary education, and from Alexandrian times on several works, long or short, were composed which consisted of cryptic allusions to them, the more obscure the better, such as the *Alexandria* of Lykophron (third or second century B.C.) and Ovid's own *Ibis*. They are simply puzzles to amuse learned readers. It is no wonder that various compendia of mythology were written at dates ranging from about the last century B.C. to the beginning of the Middle Ages, whereof several survive, and are of great utility, though only if read judiciously, for they are apt to jumble together really ancient myths and sagas with the most trifling fancies of late authors. It is a complaint of Juvenal that a schoolmaster was expected to have all manner of mythological details at his fingers' ends and be able to inform a casual inquirer about the family relations of an obscure person mentioned once in Vergil. The age had a fancy for catalogues and lists, and someone seems to have drawn up a kind of index of all the most scandalous stories about the gods, including their love-affairs. The allusions we have to it come largely from Christian writers, who pounced upon it gleefully as showing what immoral creatures the pagan deities really were. But mythological ornaments continued to be used, sometimes in rather unexpected places. For instance, in the time of Constantine VII, emperor of Constantinople (born A.D. 911), there was compiled from much older sources a work on agriculture, the *Geoponica*. It naturally consists for the most part of information concerning plants and domesticated animals, with directions, practical or superstitious, for their breeding or cultivation, but it is enlivened with several stories, some familiar (as Athena creating the first olive-tree, Narkissos and his sad end), some otherwise unknown. Thus, cypresses were once daughters of Eteokles, king of Orchomenos, who while dancing with the Charites (p. 25) tumbled into a well and were drowned. Myrtle was an Athenian girl, Myrsine, a favourite with Athena because of her interest in atheltics. She was murdered by jealous young men whose rivals she had adjudged victors and garlanded, but the plant into which she was turned remained a favourite of the goddess. Roses owe their colour and odour to the accidental spilling of a bowl of nectar, which dripped down from heaven to earth, and lilies their whiteness to some drops of Hera's breastmilk which did not go to form the Milky Way (p. 156). *Ia* (properly, it would seem, violets, but the word is used very loosely of several other kinds of flowers), were first produced by Earth as fodder for Io when she was turned into a heifer (p. 99), and ivy was once a youth named Kittos (Ivy), who was dancing in honour of Dionysos when he fell and was mortally injured. The plant still keeps his affection for the god, for it twines around grape-vines.

These examples may suffice to show how not only acquaintance with myths but apparently some rather feeble attempts to make them lingered on into the Middle Ages. Nothing like a full account can be given of the immense ramifications of some of the better-known sagas down almost to modern times, for example the extension of the story of Troy to provide a fabulous origin for Great Britain, still less of the endless satires, moral tales and other literary works which clothed their allegories in the form of myths concerning Apollo if the subject was literature, Venus if it was amorous, and so forth. Quite a large and interesting book might also be written concerning recent, indeed contemporary, retellings from various points of view of classical tales, such as the stories of Elektra and Antigone, sometimes with retention of the traditional names and places, sometimes with the old plot but a wholly modern setting. These are perfectly legitimate forms of literature, as much so as the rehandling of the themes by various ancient writers of different dates, and their existence proves how lively and interesting such products of ancient imagination were and are. But there is no room for them in a work such as this.

BIBLIOGRAPHY

The principal works on classical mythology are in German. They include:

L. Preller, *Griechische Mythologie,* vierte Auflage, bearbeitet von Carl Robert, Berlin, 1894 and later. This is an elaborate work in several volumes, admirable in its fullness and sound judgment. It is commonly quoted as 'Preller-Robert'.

W. H. Roscher, *Ausführliches Lexikon der griechischen und römischen Mythologie,* Leipzig 1884-1937. As a collection of material this is fundamental, but many of the older articles maintain opinions now seen to be groundless or at least in need of much modification. Quoted as 'Roscher's *Lexicon*'.

There are also many articles on ancient mythology and religion in *Paulys Realencyclopädie der classischen Altertumswissenschaft,* neue Bearbeitung begonnen von Georg Wissowa, Stuttgart 1894 and following years. This is an immense and extremely learned compilation, still in progress and continued after G. Wissowa's death by other scholars. The contributors are mostly but not all Germans, and include many of their best scholars. Quoted as 'Realencyclopädie', 'Pauly-Wissowa', or 'RE'.

Among shorter works the following may be found useful; I limit myself to those in English and one in French:

Pierre Grimal, *Dictionnaire de la mythologie grecque et romaine,* Paris 1951. Every article is accompanied by references to the chief relevant passages in ancient authors and a few to modern discussions. Handily indexed.

Oxford Classical Dictionary, Oxford 1949. Contains a large number of articles, mostly short, on mythology and religion.

The various encyclopedias such as the *Britannica* and *Chambers* also contain relevant articles, but generally handle the myths briefly and without much detail. The older editions of most of these works are often misleading, the authors being under the influence of theories now known to be false.

Of the many books dealing with some aspect of the subject, I mention the following:

Bacon, Janet Ruth, *The Voyage of the Argonauts,* London 1925. Brightly written, sensible and interesting.

Cook, A. B., *Zeus,* Cambridge 1914-40. A huge collection of absolutely reliable facts, accompanied by explanations often very hazardous.

Frazer, Sir J. G., *Apollodorus* (Loeb Classical Library, 2 vols.). Text and translation with valuable notes.

Same, *Fasti of Ovid,* 5 vols., London 1929. Contains translation and very full notes and discussions, including some on mythological points.

Frazer's other works, especially *The Golden Bough* (3rd ed., London 1911-36) and his large annotated translation of Pausanias (2nd ed., 6 vols., London 1913) contain incidentally a great deal of information on mythology.

Nilsson, M.P., *The Mycenaean Origin of Greek Mythology,* Berkeley, California, 1932.

Same, *The Minoan-Mycenaean Religion, 2nd ed., Lund* 1950.

Rose, H. J., *A Handbook of Greek Mythology,* 5th ed., London 1953. There is also a German translation, *Griechische Mythologie, ein Handbuch,* Munich, 1955, which has some corrections and additions not in the English editions.

Rouse, W. H. D., *Nonnos, Dionysiaca,* Loeb Classical Library, 3 vols. Text with introduction and annotated translation. Useful for those who wish to examine the late vagaries of mythology.

INDEX

Non-classical users of this index should remember that there are no silent letters in either Greek or Latin. Thus, the name Europe is of three syllables, not two; Amphitrite of four, not three. In Greek, *ai, ei, eu, oi*, are regularly dipthongs; in Latin, *æ, eu, œ*.

Since Greek mythology came to modern Europe largely through Latin authors, the Latin forms of sundry names are given here, whether present in the text or not. Romans naturally spelled them in their own fashion, writing *c* for the Greek *k* (kappa), as Circe, *ae* for *ai*, as Aeolus, *e* or *i* for *ei*, as Clio, *oe* for *oi*, as Menoeceus. They also modified the endings to suit their style of inflexion, as Pluto, not Pluton. It has already been mentioned (pp. 157ff) that they substituted their names of gods for the Greek ones. In addition, they sometimes picked up a Greek name in an unusual or corrupted form, as Ulixes (later distorted into Ulysses) for Odysseus.

Accents on proper names mark the syllables stressed in the conventional English pronunciation (generally very different from the Greek sound). If there is no accent, the first syllable is to be stressed. Principal references are in bold-faced type.

179

NEL BESTSELLERS

NEL BESTSELLERS